Jewish Grandmothers

JEWISH GRAND-MOTHERS

Sydelle Kramer and Jenny Masur, editors

With Photographs by Catherine Foley

Beacon Press   Boston

Copyright © 1976 by Sydelle Kramer and Jenny Masur

Photographs copyright © 1976 by Catherine Foley

Beacon Press books are published under the auspices
of the Unitarian Universalist Association

Printed in the United States of America

9 8 7 6 5 4 3 2 1

Library of Congress Cataloging in Publication Data

Main entry under title:
Jewish grandmothers.
    CONTENTS: Introduction: Breaking stereotypes.—
Why they came to America: Shapiro, F. The rebel.
Rothman, S. The watchmaker. Soskin, R. The hungry
child.—How they came, the passage to America:
Moscowitz, P. The child immigrant. Govsky, K. Getting
here the hard way. [etc.]
    1. Jews in Russia—Biography. 2. Jews in
Russia—Social conditions. 3. Jews in Chicago—
Biography. 4. Jews in Chicago—Social conditions.
5. Russia—Social conditions. 6. Chicago—Social
conditions. I. Kramer, Sydelle. II. Masur, Jenny.
DS135.R95A13   301.45′19′24073   75-5292
ISBN 0-8070-5420-8

So that none of these women
and no one like them
shall be forgotten

Contents

    *Pseudonyms

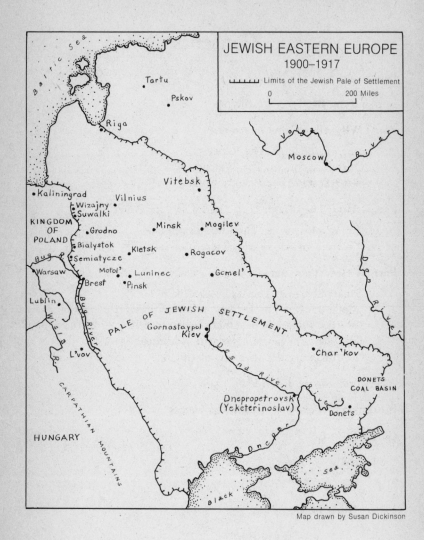

JEWISH EASTERN EUROPE
1900–1917

Limits of the Jewish Pale of Settlement

0   200 Miles

Baltic Sea

Tartu
Pskov
Riga

Volga River
Moscow

Vitebsk

Kaliningrad
Wizajny
Suwalki
Vilnius

KINGDOM
OF
POLAND

Grodno
Minsk
Mogilev

Bialystok
Kletsk
Rogacov

Bug R.
Semiatycze

Warsaw
Motol'
Luninec
Gomel'

Brest
Pinsk

Lublin

Wisla R.

Bug River

PALE OF JEWISH SETTLEMENT

Gornostaypol
Kiev

L'vov

Desna River

Char'kov

Don River

DONETS
COAL BASIN

Dnepropetrovsk
(Yeketerinoslav)

Donets

CARPATHIAN MOUNTAINS

HUNGARY

Dneper

Sea

Black

Map drawn by Susan Dickinson

A lady called me up today. She said she was in possession of her family archives. She had heard I was a writer. She wondered if I would help her write about her grandfather. . . . She offered a share of the profits, but that is something too inorganic. It would never rush her grandfather's life into any literature I could make.

The next day, my friend Lucia and I had coffee and we talked about this woman. Lucia explained to me that it was probably hard to have family archives or even only stories about outstanding grandparents or uncles when one was sixty or seventy and there was no writer in the family and the children were in the middle of their own lives. She said it was a pity to lose all this inheritance just because of one's own mortality. . . .

I thought about our conversation. Actually, I owed nothing to the lady who'd called. It was possible that I did owe something to my own family and the families of my friends. That is, to tell their stories as simply as possible, in order, you might say, to save a few lives.

Grace Paley   "Debts"   *Enormous Changes at the Last Minute*

Foreword

I suppose one could say that this project started on my grand-mother's knee, for it was there, when I was a small girl, that I first heard the stories about life and death in Russia, emigration to America, and the struggle to "make good" here. Years later, at a small feminist publishing meeting, some women and I discussed the need for some sort of book describing the experiences of our grandmothers and paying tribute, however indirectly, to their lives. The sharing of this kind of desire, and the same early fascination with our grandmothers, led Jenny Masur and me into the collaboration which produced this book. It is our hope that it will reach and affect a wide audience, and perhaps stimulate imaginations and influence self-images as much as working on it has ours.

One of the first women we talked to used to say to us, "You can't picture in your minds . . ." She was right—two American-born women could not possibly know what her generation had lived through. We cannot remember the Russian Revolution, the heartbreak of World Wars I and II, the Great Depression, or the drudgery experienced by a housewife before the advent of modern conveniences. We have not had to live in situations where we could put no faith in the people around us, as did the Jews in Eastern Europe, nor have we had to live as refugees or immigrants starting from scratch with no money or fluency in the language. It is only because of the women who shared their experiences and memories with us that we have even a glimmering of what the immigrant experience must have been like.

In addition to the women whose stories appear in this book, we would like to thank all the other women who shared their memories with us, and in doing so added to our appreciation of their generation.

We would also like to extend our sincere thanks to the following people who did so much to help and encourage us: Rabbi Daniel Leifer; Ralph Carlson; Kathleen Thompson; Ida Richter; the staff of the Drexel Home for the Aged, especially Flora Kaplan; Arcadius and Pearl Kahan; Andrea Pfeiffer; Lee Tockman; Sally Banes; Lynda Erinoff; Miriam Bazell; James Schulz; Linda Rothstein; Peter Coey;

Royann Hanson; Julie Zolot; Erica Raphael; Nancy Stetten; George-anne Marsh; Sarah Schufeldt; Paul Dilys; Dennis Melhouse; John Marino; Paul Thompson; Mrs. O. Stegman; Susan Dickinson; Mary Lou Dietrich; Kathy Barnes; Howard Kavinski; Tom Radko; Eileen Stewart; Bernard Wax; Barbara Rosenwein; and Chuck and Gus Bloom. There are many more friends and relatives to thank for their support—we trust you know who you are. Finally, special thanks must go to our editor, Roberta Fitzsimmons, who made it possible for the history of these women to come alive in book form. At all times, she shared with us a commitment to the integrity of these women and a concern for the ideas of this book.

S. K.
J. M.

Introduction   Breaking Stereotypes

This is a book about immigrants, women, Jews, and the generation of old people some of us know only as our grandparents. It is a book about the lives of Eastern European Jewish women who emigrated to this country between the turn of the century and the 1920s, a period in which streams of Jews came to America and settled in concentrated numbers in a few major cities like Boston, New York, Philadelphia, and Chicago.

We have sought in these chapters to give women an opportunity to define themselves in their own words, to reveal, through their stories and experiences, our history from the perspective of women, our roots as Americans, and our Jewish-American heritage. As Jewish women, we began with Jewish women, as much in search of ourselves as in search of them. However, one need not be Jewish to appreciate these women and learn from them.

Although all minority groups are victims of our society's propensity to stereotype, Jewish women in particular have suffered from this traditional glossing over. When they have been recognized, it has been only to face denigration. Their stereotype is multiple: one facet involves the image of women in general; another centers around the caricature of the Jew. In a sense, Jews and women are both members of the same class, the class of the oppressed, sharing minority group status in a culture which is shaped predominantly by male WASPs. Jews share with women the constant search for identity and resistance to a complete absorption by an outside culture. Jewish consciousness, like women's consciousness, is considered vital to survival. Jews have always protested the traditional stereotyping of their character which appears "even in America." More than ever before, women too are protesting against the stereotypes our society forces upon them.

Yet the Jewish fight against the Jewish stereotype does not seem to have affected the image of the Jewish woman. Jewish men are not concerned with her image, particularly that of the older immigrant Jewish woman, as a weak and ignorant loudmouth who, paradoxically, with her accented speech and exaggerated mannerisms, bullies and controls those around her. The caricature sometimes casts her as a saint, the sacrificial supermother who thrives on self-deprivation, or as the aggressive female Shylock who hoards her money while mocking the spirituality and sensitivity of her husband or son. Jewish men seem unaware that these caricatures are insulting to them as well as to women; instead they actually participate in this kind of distortion with great energy, to which many Jewish novels and stories attest.

Sholom Aleichem, perhaps, lent the stereotyping of Jewish women respectability even within the Jewish community itself. His evocation of life in the *shtetl* was so powerful and accurate to those who read him that the inadequacies of his female characters were overlooked. His women are merely sketches. In *Tevye's Five Daughters*, for example, the women are dealt with only in relation to Tevye; they are used to create situations so that Aleichem may further develop the attributes of his main character. The women exist only for Tevye to react against; each woman represents only a different facet of what might have been a full-bodied character. The result is a superficial portrait of women. *Fiddler on the Roof*, which is based on *Tevye's Five Daughters*, simplifies the women even further. Unfortunately, it is this representation of Jewish life which has reached more people than any other.

Probably the most notorious recent example of the stereotyping of Jewish women in literature is Philip Roth's novel *Portnoy's Complaint*. Sophie Portnoy is a perpetuation, albeit a brilliant one, of the convention of the Jewish mother as seen by Americans. She is everything the stereotype would have us believe: a querulous, loud, castrating, smothering inflictor of guilt. But, we see her through the eyes of her son, who admits he does not understand her, or through the eyes of the author, whose forte is caricature. This makes for a funny and often dramatic novel, but not necessarily for real and understandable characters. Roth has seized upon the most obvious elements of Jewish motherhood. While he may feel his satirization is precisely the point of his novel, because of it, his depiction of life is finally shallow. Like a stereotype itself, the novel fails to capture the full reality. It may be true that Sophie Portnoy reminds some people of women they know; but it is equally true that no one knows anyone just like her.

Older Jewish women are also often the victims of stereotypes which surround the immigrant and the elderly. Yet the resemblance of the women in this book to the prevailing stereotypes is faint. They are not ignorant—they all know several languages and are well-read, besides having learned well from experience. They are not weak—they have lived through and triumphed over the traumas of immigration, culture shock, the Depression, the deaths (sometimes murders) of members of their families, poverty, anti-Semitism, and more. They are not passive. None of the women in this book was content to stay at home and do nothing; they pursued either education or a career and by doing so broke out of the ghetto of passive domesticity for women.

They have grown old surrounded by children who know very little about their lives. Many feel they have nothing left to contribute to their society. Yet they offer us all a heritage to look back upon with pride. Now is the time to begin to learn about them—now, before their generation is gone.

After all these years of neglect, we wished to offer these women an opportunity to recount their lives in their own words, to define themselves in their own voices. We began by interviewing a variety of women in Chicago. Of our original group, we chose ten women whose lives, uniquely led, reflected the texture of an entire generation's history. We have edited their words to eliminate our questions and to arrange the flow of the whole. For a variety of reasons, several of the women asked to remain anonymous. Their histories appear with pseudonyms.

Each chapter is a refutation of stereotypes which accompany every one of us through daily life. Stereotypes try to pin something on all of us. There is no immunity based upon religion, ethnic group, age, or sex. There is a stereotype for everyone, and in remedying one, we help to remedy them all. It is our hope that readers will use this book as a springboard for insight into their own roots, and that the public imagination will be awakened to the color and quality of lives which until now have been passed over. To these women, who have contributed so much to our lives, in some cases to our very survival, we owe a history of themselves, and, by implication, their generation. To ourselves, women and men, we owe a sense of pride in those who helped to make us what we are, and the reconstruction of lives with which we should and must identify. We must be exposed to the vitality and energy of those we have been taught to ignore or patronize.

American history will never be rounded until the lives of its women, immigrants or not, belong to the public; it will stand unfinished until the experiences of its minority groups complete it; it will flow shallow until the words of its elderly deepen it. The women of this book will not speak false tribute to themselves, but rather share their lives and perceptions with us, and allow a public so long accustomed to hearing Portnoy's complaint the opportunity to read the whole story.

Finally, it is important to say that we enjoyed this project, and we think the women who shared their lives with us did as well.

May our readers appreciate and learn from them as we did.

PART ONE

Why They Came to America . . .

Yes, I make demands—not in arrogance, but in all humility. I demand—driven by my desire to give. I want to give not only that which I am, but that which I might be if only I had the chance.

—Anzia Yezierska, *Children of Loneliness*

Fannie Shapiro: The Rebel

At eighty-four, Fannie Shapiro is a personable woman and an excellent raconteur. Because of her failing health, she now lives, much to her regret, in a home for the aged on the South Side of Chicago. She misses the bustle of life "outside" and the sense of contribution gained by working.

She arrived in New York from White Russia in 1906, and stayed with an aunt in Harlem. Within three days, she had a job in a sweatshop, despite the traumas of her voyage here, and the new country and language. She was interested in giving up religion, finding out about socialism, and breaking away from her mother's limited notions of what a daughter should do; but she still thought in terms of a dowry, a Jewish identity, and motherhood.

She had grown up on an isolated estate in Russia and was eager to escape. America promised her everything she felt Russia had denied her—education, a free choice in marriage, sophistication, and financial security. While many of her expectations about America were proven false, she did find here the opportunity to have a life of her own and to be the kind of Jew, wife, and mother she wanted to be. She found three husbands and became the mother of a son and stepson.

Mrs. Shapiro is a self-styled rebel who sought her own solutions to the limitations of her life in Russia. Although America disappointed her in some ways, she is not bitter. Here, she no longer had to rebel out of frustration; she could become an independent woman.

Note: "Fannie Shapiro" is a pseudonym.

MY FATHER once picked himself up and went to America, so we lived in the house in the village then. I must have been at this time about six or seven years old. Just a one-street little place. In Jewish it's a *dorf*—a street and houses on each side and there's a place for a cow and a place for the horse and the fields and that's all. The mujiks, the peasants, lived there.

We had a house in the village. Our own home, and that was already modern. There was a pot fixed in the stove; we'd have hot water. Yes, but not much—you know, not enough for a bath. Well, it was nice. It was with two bedrooms and a living room and a dining room, kitchen. One story, sure.

Well, in those days, a lot of the fathers used to leave their families and go to America and try to establish themselves. So it used to be the style when they had a girl, to send them earrings. And that was something—from America. So, but I didn't have my ears pierced and my mother wouldn't let me. So I went to this woman and told her that my mother sent me. So she took a needle and she stuck it through my ears. And my ears got swollen and we had to call, not the doctor—he was supposed to be a doctor but he wasn't. But he knew a little. So he came and he gave me some kind of a medicine and I healed up. But then I never cared anymore for earrings.

Well, my father came to this country: a man who [had] never worked hard, who put people to work—he was the boss. He came here, they put him in a coal cellar in New York, in Harlem, to carry coal up on the third floor. So he stayed in this country about three months and picked himself up and came back. When he came back, I was so disappointed; I cried so bitter. I was already making plans to come to America, you know. I heard so much about it, you see. And he moved to this place, to this estate. So this is where I spent my youth until I came to this country.

A rich Jew had leased [it] for a number of years, and he had people run it for him.[1] My father was just like a foreman, like one of them managers. There was an office there, where they had some book-keepers, and there was a brewery. And it was a very big place. Beautiful place.

The language was peasant and I used to speak the peasant language.[2] I used to associate with peasant children. There was no school—there was a church. They came on Sunday and went to church. And the priest used to antagonize them against Jews—of course anti-Semitism. The children used to be so bad against us; but if we could give them an apple or a slice of white *challeh*, everything was okay because they didn't have that and it was an awful lot to them. So sure, the dogs run after you and if you had a piece of that white bread and hand it to the dog even, he would leave you alone; to him it was something, too.

We lived very good, comparing with other poor people. You came to the town, and saw the way the poor people lived there, and I used to come back and tell my mother. You know, to think of something—we had a big orchard, fruit of all kinds, falling off the trees, and the peasants didn't have anything in that village. We used to have two men walking around all night watching that the peasants shouldn't break in and steal fruit. We used to sleep all summer in tents out in the orchard. My father would build up a fence and nice fresh-cut hay, and cover with a sheet and then we'd go and sleep in the tent.

The house was actually in the orchard, right at the end. We had nuts growing there, and grapes and strawberries. And there was a lake where we could catch fresh fish. All during the week, we'd have all kinds of butter and cheese, and everything that you get from the cow, everything; and then sometimes, my mother would cook some fish, and for the weekend, then we had chicken. For the weekends, we'd have to take a couple of chickens to the town, to the *shochet* to have to kill 'em. Then we'd bring 'em back and we'd pluck 'em and *kosher* them, and then we'd eat chicken.[3] Oh we ate, we ate good. Maybe this is why I'm still around, 'cause I had a hard life here.

And we lived in a house, it's sort of like a palace, considering that time—with a lot of equipment in German style. That Polack was very wealthy. We lived modern already 'cause we had one of those—it wasn't a stove. You'd open it up and put in a big log of wood and light it and tighten, screw it up, and that would keep like steam, keep heat. Oh we

had a very very nice place. Big place; and then, came on Fridays, my
mother would call in the peasant woman. She'd give her a *challeh*, and
she would wash those floors—oh, the floors—and after they got washed,
we'd cover it with sand.[4] Ooh, if you can see it, then you'd have an
idea what kind of a life it was. Leave the sand overnight so the floor
would dry up and keep—look beautiful. Plain wooden floor, but a
nice wood.

To picture the sort of life there. The young [peasant] kids got up,
they used to take care of the pigs, take care of the sheep, take care of
the chickens, ducks, and what not. But they never knew that they needed
an education; and those that did go to this church school, it was only
about three or four months during the winter; otherwise they had to
work in the fields.

There were no *pogroms*. There were a few Jewish families, and those
peasants, a lot of them made a living from those Jewish people. Like
where I lived—there were about maybe one hundred peasants employed and those who worked by day, they'd have to cut the grass there,
or cut the corn, the rye. They'd get about fifteen cents a day, and that
meant money to them that time, you know; it's so many years back.
But there was anti-Semitism all over. I used to come into the peasants'
homes, and they'd be talking amongst themselves that "the Jews live
better, the Jews live off your hard work, and the Jews educate their
children." Sometime if I'd walk through that town, boys would say:
"The *Zhid*."

There was only one school, a school where a priest in the church was
teaching. I could have gone to that school; he said he didn't mind—he
knew my father. But I'd be afraid; I had to pass through a little woods
and all the Gentile boys used to go that way, too; they'd kill me. Girls
didn't go to school at all; it was just the boys that used to go to learn a
little bit to sign their names, but to figure 2 and 2 they could never. So
the *galach*, you know, was teaching them the language and anti-Semitism at the same time.

The big cities it was different. There were schools; they had more of
a chance. But we, where I come from, there was no chance.

We used to have a *rabbi* home. He was actually a teacher. He knew
the Russian language, Hebrew, and Jewish. The Russian language
appealed to me so much.

He stayed with us; that's the way it used to be because his home was
always farsome away, some country place that you can't picture in

your mind what they looked like—primitive, you know. So we had
to have room for him. He stayed for a certain term; like when he came
beginning of the winter, he stayed till close to Passover. And then, sometime, he'd come for the summer and stay a few months; and then come
the Jewish holidays, he'd go home. I don't know if you can call it
education but it was important.

After a while my mother thought I had enough, I didn't need any
more education. That was getting me angry and that was when I started
planning quietly to come to America for an education. My father
thought I didn't have enough, but my mother. . . . But the boys,
they never had enough; my two brothers went in the village to *cheder*,
they had to take up a higher education, the kind that's not for girls—
Gemara. They were young kids, they were younger than I. I was the
oldest.

When my brothers went to school, I was home helping my mother,
and then by the time I turned around, I started getting ready to go to
America. There were other children—we were six of us. So I had to
help her. I had to help her wash laundry. You can't picture in your
mind how laundry was washed in that place; you can't. It's impossible
to explain it. You got to go and see it. I had to help her with a lot of
things and she used to watch that I don't do anything wrong with *flayshig* and *milchik*.[5]

Well, my life was entirely different than the life here. My mother was
a very primitive little woman, religious and naive like a child. And
somehow, I don't know why, I never took her serious, her religion.
On Saturdays, she'd open up one of the religious books, and it was in
Hebrew—she didn't understand Hebrew and she'd read it and she'd
cry. I knew more about religion that she did, but I somehow wasn't
religious.

Did you ever see when they light those candles on Friday night? My
mother would want me to light one candle, a girl, and *bentsh*, pray
over the candle, and I didn't want to.[6] And she'd feel very bad, so I'd
have to do it not to hurt her. But I thought, "One day I'm gonna leave
this place and you're gonna never see me again, and I am not gonna
light the candles." So she used to always say to my father—"This is
gonna grow up a *shiksa*. Someday maybe she's gonna convert herself
to the Christian religion or marry a *shaygetz*." She thought if not
Jewish, a religion you gotta have, see.

My mother went to *mikveh*.[7] She used to every month—we were not

far from that village where there was a *mikveh*. When a woman gets
her monthly, after she's got through, she's not allowed to have sex,
intercourse, unless she goes. [One time] my grandmother forgot [and
they had intercourse anyway]. So my grandfather took it to heart and
he started fasting [in penance]; he fasted so long he died.

Oh, my mother was religious, she was very religious. The summer
before I left she had to go to Bialystok, to a doctor. And I had to take
over the housework. And I didn't care—*milchik*, *flayshig*. I cooked,
I made [things in the wrong pots], and when I got through I kind of
felt funny. So I told my father. So my father says to me, "Wash all
these pots. Put them right back where you took 'em, and never tell
her anything. Forget it. It's okay." I used to quietly follow in my
father's footsteps. I used to observe everything he did.

I looked like a *shiksa*. One time an old man came to my grandmother's house, peddling. I ran in, barefoot, redhead; my grandmother
takes me in her lap and kisses me, and this old man says, "You ought
to be ashamed of yourself. You lived so long with these peasants that
you even love the peasant children." So she says, "That's my granddaughter." It so happened I had to be a redhead.

My mother used to always worry. A Jewish girl at that time, a redhead, they couldn't even get a *shiddach* for me. It would be very hard,
they'll have to have a lot of money to buy a husband. It would happen
to me the same thing as happened to others if you did have a hundred
dollars. You got married, [he] took the money, and he left you right
away to America. Sometime he sent for you, sometime he found somebody else that he liked better, and forgot you. Sent you a divorce.[8] All
of this here I took in my mind and I says, "I'm gonna run away from
here if I have to walk."

They started having problems with me; I'm a renegade, I'm reaching
sixteen or fifteen, what's gonna be, no money, how they gonna buy a
husband, *nadan*, a dowry.[9] At that time my brothers already left for
the city to go to the *Talmud Torah*. So, I says well, if they can send them
to the big city—"I am going to America, big city my eye!" So they
won't let me. Sometime I used to think I'd run away but where will I
run? I never saw a city. There was a little town not far from us, and
there's a railroad way far away. I used to see once in a while a train, and
then all the peasants used to run look at it—such a great wonder.

So I says, "I'm gonna go to the next city—call it a 'city,' and I'm gonna become a servant girl and save up money and I'm gonna go to America." City—there was a couple of houses that there were two floors. Two floors! It was the first time I saw that. And my people wouldn't let me go because at that time somehow, socialism and many other progressive things were coming to life. My father wouldn't like his daughter to become a servant girl.[10] But we had some relatives in that place; I went there, and I worked. I was with them for about a year and one half.

There was no money in it. They might have paid you about fifteen rubles a year, so was that money? But I wanted to meet young people and Jewish people. There was a teacher [in the town] who was teaching Russian, and he was a progressive person. I went to him; I made up with this woman that she even pay me less but I'm gonna take like about three hours a week. He was a socialist, but I didn't understand socialism. I didn't come in contact with the socialist movement because I didn't live in a city. I didn't see any civilization; so, I picked up on a part of it, but I really didn't know the amount of meaning of it. The only thing he taught was some of those songs—actually just a few words. At the time, you know, Russia was sort of having on her revolution. There used to be a song and I can never forget it: "Pick yourself up, workers of the world, and fight for your rights." That appeals to me so much.

Anyway, my mother when she heard this, she says, "We're gonna take her home, I don't want her to be in the city, she'll become a socialist and drop religion, no, not my daughter." So my father came and said to me one day, "Come home for *yontif*!" So I didn't want to. I understood then that my father was with me, but he didn't want to show it to me because he didn't want to hurt my mother. [And they took me back home.]

In the spring, I started to write letters to my mother's family in New York—my aunts and uncle in America—and tell them that my father and mother want to let me go (but they wouldn't); and when the letters came back and asked whether it's true, I'd read the letters the way I wanted to. They couldn't read Jewish, neither one of them, written; see, they could only read the print. They couldn't write Jewish either one of them. I told them that my aunt is asking me to come to this country.

I saw [another] aunt of mine, and she was about twenty-two—she lived in one of these peasant towns with her father and mother. And she was there alone between all these *goyim*; you'd have to go to the city to find a husband for her, and you'd have to have money to buy him. And then an old man came from the next little somewhere, and he was pretty well off, also living in one of these peasant little places. And he wanted to marry this girl. When I saw him, that old man, of maybe fifty years old, fat and filthy and dirty, and he had his own home, he was well-off, he offered everything; and that was what used to happen, these girls used to marry. And the parents started forcing her and she wouldn't marry him. She said, "If you're not gonna let me alone, I'm gonna hang myself." Well, one day she pretty near hung herself, she was so disgusted with life. Well, the end was, she too went to America.

So, when all of this happened, my mother was afraid to press too much on me. I says, "If you're not gonna let me go to America, I'm gonna drown myself. I'm not gonna go on living over here with the peasants." We had a big big lake right near the house. So my parents couldn't do anything with me, they had to let me. And I told my parents, "I want to go to America. I want to learn, I want to see a life, and I want to go to school." I used to keep all the time thinking: But how am I gonna live? What am I gonna do? All right, I'll come to family.

Costed thirty dollars for the ship, so my father wouldn't give me the money so they sent me the money from my mother's family, and I had to pay them off. When I came, they showed me the bill, and they said, "See, when you start working, you have to pay a dollar a month on this to pay that off."

So then my mother cried so bitter, "Our little girl, our *kind*, picking herself up and leaving home and daring, daring." My father took me to the train, and he cried. But he understood that I was right.

I came to Germany, to Hamburg. I stayed about a week or longer. I saw electric lights and I saw streetcars; and everything was so shocking to me by the time I got there. The first time on the train.[11]

And you got in that ship—I can't describe it to you, the filth; old and dirty and filthy. And you had to walk three floors down, on the bottom there. It was something undescribable. First day, I have to get to the steerage, all the ways down, so I didn't know how to get down there. I had a little valise in my hand, and I was sitting and crying. So a man comes over, with a beard, an old man, and he must have come from

Galicia.[12] He was saying, "Little girl, why are you crying?" So he
called over a sailor and the sailor took me and showed me where it
was. The cots were one on top of another—three, I think, and I was on
the very top one. If I had to go now on that kind of a ship, I don't think
I'd make it.

I was so innocent of sex—my mother never told me anything. And
it happened that I got my first period pretty late and I didn't know
what it was. Well, when I came to this country, I first found out things,
what it meant. It's funny: the first time I got the period, was before I
left for America. So I got scared to death, I was afraid to tell my
mother that she won't let me go. Well, when I came to this country,
my aunt asked me. She knew better. After all, I thought I was gonna
have a baby. That sailor sat on my lap, and I was so embarrassed. [I
thought he made me pregnant]. And then, he gets up and walks away
and comes back with a banana. I didn't know what it was so I take it
and throw it in the ocean. And he's laughing.[13]

Well, when I came off the ship—at that time, there was a lot of
prostitution going on in the United States, 1906. And they used to pick
up girls from the ship and take them to Argentina, to different countries, if they were nice looking. I wasn't pretty, but healthy; and you
know, I thought maybe I'd fit for the game. So an uncle of mine was
supposed to pick me up. And this uncle, when he was in the Old
Country, he had a beard—he looked like an old man and he wasn't
old. Here he was shaving, he dressed pretty nice. I didn't recognize
him.[14] And he comes to the gate, and they open the gate and call his
name and mine, and I wouldn't go. So the man who was standing there,
he asked me, "Do you know him?" I said, "No." And he says to me in
Jewish, "Don't be afraid. Come with me. I'm your uncle Isaac." Well,
I was shivering; but I went. And then I came to his house. I pictured
to myself, America, a big house. And he had three or four children and
a three room apartment and two boarders. And when I saw all of this,
I says, "What did I come to? Is that America?"

But I didn't live with this uncle because I had my mother's sister so
I stayed with her. They had a candy store and in back of the store there
was one little room, no windows.[15] And I slept in that kitchen—no bed,
no bath. Just a toilet, and if you had to take a bath, so you took a bath
in the washtub.

[The neighborhood] was mixed, and those Gentiles that lived around the Jews, they too were immigrants. You see, I came to people, they were poor themselves—immigrants. They couldn't speak English. They had a paper stand by the candy store. I had to get up five in the morning and open the store, and get myself ready to go to work. Meanwhile people would come buy the paper. My aunt, she was here for years—she couldn't read. So I said no, this wouldn't go, I had to read to know what I'm selling.

Oh, I had pictures of I would come to this country, I go right to school. Whoever thought of working? So well, I came to America, I only saw New York. Harlem. I thought to myself, "I don't blame my father that he went back." A man buys a coal cellar: you can't picture, imagine it. Buys a coal cellar, lives in the coal cellar, eats there and sleeps there, carries a pack of coal to the fifth floor for five cents, and out of that he has to make a living and save a couple of dollars to bring his family to the United States.

I was so naïve and my whole hope [was] that I was coming to this country to get an education. I didn't realize—I didn't understand how things are. I heard so much about America—a free country for the Jews, and you can get an education and you didn't have to pay for schooling, so I came. I didn't think, I didn't know. I never saw anybody working, I didn't know what it was all about; so I thought that I'll stay with the family. I'll help probably in the house, with the children, wash the dishes, and I'll go to school. But it didn't work out that way.

I came in on a Saturday, and Monday I had to go and look for a job. I come up for a job, [they set] me down by a machine and they show me how to operate it; and I take a little while to learn. [In Russia] I used to come to the small town and they had these little shops—two, three, four, or five girls in a house, working, making dresses and things. And they had a Singer's, a sewing machine. I used to envy [them]; the girls would be sitting and working and singing; I thought it was so much fun. Singing. God, I didn't think it was anything serious.

[Here] you're not allowed to talk to each other. And you had, I think, about fifteen minutes for lunch and I'd have to take along something from home, but I could buy an apple for a penny. Where I come from I never knew I had to pay a penny for an apple. I was getting about $1.95 or something like that for six days work, sixty hours.

And little by little I tried to pick up the language as best as I could. And working in a shop, hardly anyone spoke English. All Yiddish;

the shop belongs to a Jewish man and all the workers were Jewish. They were all just immigrants, immigrants, immigrants.

And all you can hear [are] these who are a short time in this country and they thought they were Americans and they call me and others the *grueneheim*. And my aunt and my uncle—I was here about a few months, if she had to go downtown, I had to take her. And she used to call *me* the grueneheim.[16]

Then I thought to myself I'm gonna work another while and I'm gonna go out look for a job, and see what I can accomplish. So I met up with a girl. We went to look for a job together. We went up and found a job. We worked partners, and we made each six dollars a week. I had to leave the shop on account of the boss pinched me. One day the machine—those old machines—broke; I had to get up on the table to reach it. So when I went up on the table reaching and the boss, an old man, he went and he pinched me so I gave him a crack and he fell. He was very embarrassed; so the whole shop went roaring. He thought I would keep quiet. I was so naive, I thought a man touched me—so he fired me. He told me, "Get out, greenhorn." He was right, not I.

So I come home and tell my uncle and aunt. So they told me that where the *Forward*'s building was —there's a lawyer has an office and he takes care of these kind of cases.[17] So I come, and the first thing, I had to throw in a dime in a box and I didn't have the dime; so anyway he lets me come in. And then he started asking me have I got parents here. He was a very nice Jewish guy. Then I had to tell him exactly what happened. He says, "I'm gonna send them a law letter. If he sends you the money, fine; if not you'll have to go to court and tell them exactly what happened." I couldn't sleep nights. How am I gonna come in a court and tell the judge? Finally he sent me my five dollars. So I tell you.

Then I started looking around for other jobs, and I went and registered at night school. And night school was about six or seven blocks away, and I never got home before seven. So I take a bite, and run to night school; I was so anxious to learn. And when I came to night school, I was so tired, after all, I'd fall asleep there. So I had to give up; I went and I bought one of these translators and I used to [learn with it], after washing all the diapers and all the dishes and going to bed and getting up.

Then I got tired of this kind of life with them. I started earning a little more money. I moved out. There was such a scandal in the family; I tell you—uncles and aunts; boy, they wrote to my parents that I moved to strangers and my parents were so worried about it. I moved out to strangers, to strangers. I mean, I worked in a shop with a girl, we became friends, and so she said she has a room all to herself, so we can share it, and I wouldn't have to pay much.

There I met people my own age; we formed a Jewish club, we played theater, and we danced. None of us had any talent, but we just got together, and life was different. I worked a little shorter hours that time. It was an entirely different life I started living.

I did get involved with unions—the Ladies Garment Workers Union [ILGWU].[18] Maybe by about two or three years later, I came into a shop and he asked me for a union book. I told him I didn't belong. So he told me, "If you join the union, you can get a job." I went to the union, and the union told me, "If you get a job, we'll give you a union book. Quick, get a job." See, that's the way it works. So finally I got a job one place and it was a union shop, and somebody who worked in that place helped me and I finally got a union book. I joined the union. Just think of it: working ten hours a day for any price the boss wanted to give you. You had nothing to say. But when the union came in, he couldn't do it. You very rarely worked in one shop for a long time 'cause if you asked for a raise, if he didn't think you deserved it, he fired you. So, well, I was fired and I went lookin' for a job, and I found a job.

When I came into that place to work, it happened the shop chairlady was getting married, so she can't work. There was nobody who could take the job because [no one could] speak the little English that I could speak and write. So I took this temporarily, and I worked there about six years. And I was the shop chairlady. When you're shop chairlady, you belong to the union, you have to come to report to the union. Sometimes a strike came up. You have to go on the stage and take the floor and explain what's happening. Oh, then the union was a Jewish union and Jewish men. Yes, and I got married from that place.

There were all kinds of strikes. We picketed. [One] strike took a long time. The police gave us a taste of the club. One day there was a fight between the strikers and the scabs and the policemen—and we were arrested. So on the way to one of these big police wagons, I kept begging the policeman to let me off. I said, "The judge don't want to see me; my little boy wants to see me. Let me go home." So there was a lucky break. There were so many, because the entire trade was striking (it's not only one shop), so when we came in, the judge says, "What'd you bring me another horde for? Where am I going to put them? I don't want them." And he started screaming at the policeman. Quietly —my name wasn't on anywhere—I snuck out, and I went home to my little boy. I come home and my little boy saw me, he says, "I wouldn't let you go to work anymore. Maxie's mother don't work. She stays home. I want you to stay home too."

Finally we settled. We got a raise. And as time went on, we kept on getting raises until the end. I got fifty dollars a week and I think forty hours, worked five days.

I hated to leave. After I was making such a nice money, I hated to leave. My husband pestered me. I've gone through plenty of hell in my life but this is the most interesting. When I was gonna leave, my boss almost cried because they always had trouble with the shop chairlady, with the other people who were supposed to be big shots. But all the time I was shop chairlady, everything worked out pretty nice. I used to love to work. I wish I did now.

In my case (I was so eager for education I couldn't get), I met up with a man, he had schooling, went to public school. He spoke English and I thought he was very educated. I thought I was getting a bargain but I fooled myself. He was Americanized, see, that was the most important. And he seemed to be a nice person.

So I got married. He was a cigarmaker and he was making very little, so I gave him a proposition. First thing I told him, "Let's not have any babies. Let's both work and let's make as much as we can— earn and save up some money (how much money did you need at that time?), and I want to take a trip and see my parents and my home and my brothers and sisters. I want to help them come to this country, I want to do whatever I can."

So he agreed about everything, and of course I didn't know. I was naive to life and he was older than I and he knew more than I did. So before I looked around, I gave birth to my baby, and did I have a struggle until I was able to go back to the shop to work and leave him with a friend. And you know, at first, I had to go home at night and I didn't know what to do first. I struggled for some time until my boy was about six years old. I got tired of this kind of a life. I said to myself,

"He's not trying anything"—I was making then already more than he did. I told him, "I want to break up with you," and I did. I divorced him and I took the boy with me. I was working and I gave up my little home. I went and I lived with some friends.

Comparing with my mother, I was already a civilized mother. I saw things different. I saw how children were being brought up, and it was altogether different. My little boy went to the school when he was at the age of six; there was a school right across the street. I never poked religion into his mind. He knew he was Jewish, but we have to be human beings and get along with everybody and understand things, I mean, and be respectable.

Well, this man wanted to marry me but I made up my mind I'm not gonna get married. After I got rid of my [first] husband and thought through all my troubles, I promised myself not to marry, just to stay single. I'm earning a living now and I have a good job and I am a shop chairlady. I'm gonna raise my boy and give him an education. If I get married, I won't be able to do it. I used to like to work; I hated to tie myself down to the house. Those days when you got married, you stay home and you become a housewife and start making babies. Like they all had a houseful. Did I hate that, because the circumstances did not allow for such large families.

Well, that man was after me about four years and one day I told him, "I'm not gonna get married, I'm not gonna marry you." So he picked himself up and left his boy with these people that I lived with. He had some connection here in business in Chicago. He stayed about two months, he came back, he says, "Now we're getting married," I says, "Okay." I like him but I thought I'm gonna sacrifice. Maybe my child will never get an education.

And when I married I told him, I says, "We got the two boys. We're not youngsters anymore. There's one thing. We have no *right* to have any more children. We have to give these children an education. We owe them an awful lot." I devoted my very moment to my little boy and his boy.

And the second marriage I didn't have to work. He was making good money, he himself worked hard, and I had to be home; we were a family of four, and somebody had to take care of things. We led really a happy life. He was pretty well off in business, he fixed up a beautiful home in Boro Park. All the middle class live there.

I married a man who liked music, who was an intelligent man. He wasn't religious, no. That guy was so independent, he was from the Old Country, one of those scholars of Hebrew.[19] He was a lovely person and he took me places that I all my life wanted to but I couldn't get; he always come home with tickets to the opera, tickets to this, tickets to that.

Everything was fine for about three years and then the Depression— well, we had to give [up] everything and then he went to Chicago and we came her we struggled a little bit and then he made a living here. The boys were already in college. Well, his son graduated Northwestern but mine made only two years. He had to work.

Then my husband was in the decorating business, painting. So, things are pretty hard and we moved into a building that had belonged to Czechoslovaks. So they didn't employ Jews, anti-Semitic. While we were living there we were struggling, and we couldn't pay our rent. We owed them about two or three months' rent. The rent was about $35/month—four-room apartment. So one day the agent comes and says to me, "I am sorry, I'm sorry. We're gonna have to get you out of here. I hate to do it because you people are nice."

I says, "I'm gonna go down to the office and I'm gonna talk to Mr. Whatever-his-name-was (I forgot)." My husband was too independent, he wouldn't do it, wouldn't lower himself. I didn't tell him anything. I went down to this office and I talked to this Mr. Whatever-his-name-was and I told him, I says, "We owe you for three months' rent. I'm not asking for anything but give my husband a chance to work off the three months' rent so that we wouldn't be thrown out, and we wouldn't be owing you anything. That's all I ask for." He says, "Send him around. I want to talk to him."

So my husband went down there, and he immediately gave him three or four apartments, to go and see and give him an estimate. So he gave him this estimate and he gave him work; these checks put us on our feet and he started making a good living and we traveled, we went wintertime to Florida, we went to California, we went to Hot Springs, Arkansas. And I tell you we had a wonderful life. We fixed up a nice home; then all of a sudden, he took sick—cancer in the spine— and struggled in the hospital and home and finally died.

So, I made up my mind. I'm gonna stay single and I went back to look for a job. I worked for a while here and there. Meanwhile the boys got married and had families. And then I got to know in one of the shops, a woman, a friend. And she had a brother who was divorced. And she started talking me into marrying her brother. And I didn't want to get married, but it was hard for me to work for a living in the factory. I didn't care too much for him, but about two or three years later, I married this man; otherwise, I couldn't have got Social Security. So I married him in January; in June he gets a heart attack, going to work he had it. He was a sign painter and with the ads and offices he was making good. As far as money goes, it was fine—and he was a nice man.

So it's twenty years since I'm alone. I couldn't go back with the shop anymore. I was tired out. So I used to do home alterations, and then I was already getting Social Security.

But recently, you know, I started figuring out I'm gonna be eighty-four and I couldn't take care of things the way I did; and I was getting very tired, and I couldn't do this and I couldn't [do that]. I saw what happened to some of my friends—they broke down. You can't get a doctor home, and I was under a doctor's care all the time for my blood pressure. Sometime I don't feel too good. I don't know; I don't think I could have held out for another year because it was hard for me to do things, very hard. You see, I may not look my age, but I feel it. So I tell you, I figured this way. I'm pretty close to eighty-four. What happens when I get sick? Things are so expensive. You get into the hospital, you need thousands of dollars.

Well, over here [in the Home], it's a different thing altogether. My Social Security card—I don't even know how much I'm getting now 'cause I don't have to know. When I moved in here, they were so cold to me. Not one of them even talked to me with the exception of about three of them on this floor. I didn't know how to get around, how to do—I was lost. I says, "What did I do? I gave up my little home." So you see, it's not to say that I am too happy.

Sarah Rothman: The Watchmaker

Sarah Rothman was one of the few women in Eastern Europe in the early 1900s to have a trade—she was a watchmaker. Because of her trade, she was the envy of her peers and neighbors. However, her trade brought with it enormous financial responsibilities—as a child she found herself the major means of support for her family. As a result she developed an individuality and pragmatic decisiveness which have carried her through war and personal crises.

At eighty-one, Mrs. Rothman is a woman who refused at all times to be passive about her life. Although she was a married adult with a successful business, she unhesitatingly emigrated to this country. Her decision was not based on financial considerations (as was that of many other immigrants); rather, she was concerned about the safety of her husband, whom she had loved enough to marry in defiance of her father's wishes. She married her first cousin. In America, when she learned of the genetic risks involved, she refused to have more children; she even had an illegal abortion.

In contrast to her husband's radical political commitments, which she respected, Mrs. Rothman's most vital commitments have always been familial; but she did picket for her union and has worked with Women for Peace. She has never been content to sit back and not contribute to her livelihood in some fashion.

Mrs. Rothman is a woman who defines herself through personal relationships—without being submissive to anyone. She is a woman who has managed to combine independence with romance.

Note: "Sarah Rothman" is a pseudonym.

I WAS THINKING, if I could only write a book, I would have so much to tell. We were a poor family. My mother wanted to go to *shul*, but she didn't have nice clothes and she was kind of embarrassed. The roof was leaking. My father was a sick man, and he worked very little. He died young. And I was the supporter of the whole family; I was the oldest. I started to learn the trade of watch repairing when I was very young—ten years old. I was mechanically inclined. I started making money when I worked for my grandfather (my mother's father) as a watch repairer; and I took care of [him and] the house. I used to make a meal for him—eleven years old.

My grandfather was also a rabbi. When a Gentile used to have trouble with a partnership with a Jew, they used to trust my grandfather that he's just. The regular *rabbi* used to say to him, "You know, you know more *Talmud* than I do." They used to come to him—they killed a calf, and the calf is *trayf*. You know that he used to make it *kosher*. You know why? Some people are sick; they are very poor, they had no money to buy meat. Then he overlooked. He used to look at the book [*Talmud*] and used to say this is *kosher*. He used common sense.[1]

When my grandfather died, I took over the business. And I had a big sign, the dial of a big clock, on my house on top of the door—WATCH REPAIR. Before he died, he says, "Well, I'm dying. And I want you to have all the tools and the equipment." When he said good-bye to me, he put his hands on my head—oh, I'll never forget—and I cried. I says, "Grandpa, you're leaving. How will I be able to take care? I don't have enough experience to open a shop." All kinds of watches that I didn't know how to take apart. He says, "You will learn. You'll break plenty watches." And I did break a lot of them. I was trying. He was ninety-four years old. I used to cry, "I couldn't fix, I didn't learn enough. What should I say? I'll say the watch is not working—I broke it? What should I tell them, what should I tell them? How can I get them back the watches? Before it used to work a little bit, but now it's not working altogether." What I went through, I don't know why I'm living that long, I'm telling you. I broke plenty of watches. I used to feel so bad, you know, especially from a poor man that had no money to buy another.

My customers were mostly those that were working for the offices; managers, you know, working for the rich landowners—mostly Gentiles. They thought because they saw so many watches hanging, people are trusting her, she must be good. I used to tell them, "You know, if the watch is not going to run, if anything is wrong before a year is over, I won't charge you anything unless you drop it. Then it's not my fault." (You could tell if it comes from a fall, like a doctor knows how [sickness] is developed.)

It didn't bother [the customers that I was a woman]. You know how it is—they needed me so badly. Many times [a customer would say], "I want the watch to be fixed in my presence. I'll sit here and I'll watch you." I took the watch apart and he used to shake—"My God, an expensive watch. Will you be able to get it together the way it was before?" I said, "If I wouldn't, I wouldn't undertake it." I sure was [nervous]. If they say something bad about me, the whole office would know; I would lose a lot of trade.

To fix a watch, a ruble was the highest [price]. It was a lot of work; I had to show him that I put jewels inside. I would charge him for material and labor. [For material] I used to send to Warsaw; by mail, it takes four weeks.

I made more money than some men. I was the only watchmaker in town: that's why I could have charged them as much as I want. Those that have watches as the memory from their father or from their mother, or bought it for a *bar mitzvah* and it's so dear to him—he didn't care, he would pay as much as you would tell him. They figured that another watchmaker, a man, that has to make a living for a family would charge them more than I did. I charged them less.

I made a living. With that money, when the roof was leaking, I had to hire a man to come fix it. Otherwise, the water used to come down in your bed. We used to have pots and dishes full of water.

My mother used to take care of the house, used to cook, used to shop, used to clean. My mother was not too well and my father was sick most of the time. His heart was very bad. They were the same age, but three times the czar's army tried to take him. That's why he died so young. When it came to go for a physical, he used to stay up nights not to sleep and eat Epsom salts the heart it should affect because the army for a Jew was terrible.[2]

My father wasn't considered a good match. My mother was already twenty-six years old and that was considered old, and she didn't want to remain alone. She was afraid she'll never marry and that's a disgrace. And she figured that she'll get used to him. He was a smart man, but they had nothing in common. When she married my father, he wasn't educated in Russian but he was educated in the higher *Talmud*. My mother was more modern. She used to read a book in Russian; my father used to say, "What—in Russian?"[3]

My grandfather, my father's father, used to say, "She'll be able to bear children not knowing the language or not knowing much. A woman should stay away from school." But my mother used to read for the whole block every Saturday. Was a different life altogether. Saturday and Sunday, my mother used to read the history of the Jewish people to a whole bunch of women—neighbors, relatives—in the house.[4] They used to look up to her. She was so educated in history. They used to say [to me], "You come from good stock." She was a teacher. She used to get a class of children—about eight to ten boys and girls—and she used to read the Jewish history and they used to pay her five rubles a month, very little. And if the people couldn't pay, she used to let them stay in class anyway. "She's good and she will make it up." She taught me how to read and write.

She used to talk to [men] about politics, and they used to listen; "Your mother, oy, it's a pleasure to talk to her." And my father used to make fun of her: "Eh, what are you going to talk to them about?" You know how it is—he was very religious, a *Hasid*.[5] My mother was more modern but she was very afraid that people will talk. You were under a lot of pressure at that time. In a small town—three hundred people —you didn't want criticism. What you're going through for public opinion, don't ask. Each and every one knows what anybody's doing. Couldn't eat bread on *Pesach*.[6] If someone had a fight with his wife, the whole town would talk about it.

My mother went through a lot, and then the kids didn't stop coming. I was the third one, but two died before; that's why they were so happy that I was alive. [The others died because] in the morning, it used to be so cold in the house and when you bathe them, they caught a cold and you couldn't save them.

My father inherited from his father a house. It had [a roof of] shingles and [walls] of wood. The floor wasn't the right way fixed—one board is higher than the others. We just had a couch and a table and chairs, that's all, in the front. We had one bedroom rented to get taxes, to a couple with a couple kids. That left another two bedrooms. I can't describe to you how life was. You can't imagine how people lived. We used to sleep many times in the cold weather on top of the oven; put old coats, pillows there, and sleep because it used to be so cold in the house.

Some people were envying us because we had our own production. We had a garden, we had a cow, which not everybody had, you know. We had milk. Through the calf, we used to have leather for shoes. The butter we used to sell, naturally; we couldn't afford to eat butter. My mother used to weigh it—if it's a pound, it's all right; if it's not a pound, we're going to eat. To churn it was a big bother, believe me. The top of the milk is for butter, the bottom is for sour cream or for cottage cheese. The cheese we used to put in a little sack, tie it up and have it stay hanging; and then knock it, the cheese should taste better. You have no idea how much work it is. We used to have grease for the wheels of the peasants' wagons, and flour. We give him the flour and he used to bring mushrooms, food for the chickens. We used to hire the peasant to fix up the garden; my father used to pay with honey.

We always had by us an open house. We had baked potatoes, cabbage, eggs, and they used to come in—relatives and friends. We had a barrel of herring in the wintertime. We used to make *kasheh*, *krupa* in the morning. My father used to say, "My God! What are you eating— Russian food? Why don't you eat Jewish foods?" I says, "What's the difference?" We used to speak Russian in the street.

They used to envy me, especially the girls, because I had a chance to meet so many fellows. I used to ask them to, "Come over; I'll introduce you to some that are coming for their watches." They used to have a good time. They come to my house and I used to have them like a party—meet so and so, meet so and so.

I had so many proposals. I had my choice, you understand. I wouldn't mind not to marry at all, but I had my choice. It was because

I used to make so much money. It's not only the watch repair. I used to make money selling watches, taking in exchange and get more than the watch is worth, fixing gramophones. My father wanted me to marry a religious boy like he is. He would go with him to the synagogue every day to pray. I says, "No, I'm not made for that." I was revolting.

I was corresponding with a Gentile fellow. [I met him] at the meetings. He was a Socialist. First, I belonged to the Zionists.[7] They wouldn't arrest you for being a Zionist. When Nikolai was czar, we met secretly. Later, we rented a hall. Then we had freedom. I belonged there because it was a place to get together and talk and read, girls and boys. We used to have fun. Later on, I used to belong to the Socialists. And [that Gentile boy] wrote me a beautiful letter that he came to fix the watch in order to see me again and talk to me.

Oy, that's all I need, my father would get a hold of that letter. "We should meet in Kiev," he wrote me in Russian. And I took that letter right away and I burned it up. I liked him; very nice boy. At that time, Jews and Gentiles—when they threw the czar down, we used to kiss each other: we are all brothers, we are all sisters.[8] See how it turned out. Jews specially were so happy, but my father says to me, "You'll see what's going to happen, you'll see later."

I got married at twenty-five. The parents used to worry; they have a daughter twenty-five years old. In a small town, you have no chances to meet somebody else. And the boys couldn't make a living. It's considered old, twenty-five years old, in the Old Country. If you're not in love with anybody, through a matchmaker most of them used to meet. Matchmakers used to come and talk to my father in the synagogue: "Oy, you got a very nice daughter. And why not marry, he's got a windmill, he's got a business by himself." I never believed in that. A girl could marry her father's brother or her mother's brother. Very common because you don't have to give a dowry.[9]

My husband was my first cousin. They didn't live in our town. [At first] we weren't talking to each other on account of my father didn't talk to his [my husband's] mother. We didn't go to his house.

[Before we got married], my husband was with the Bolsheviks. He used to talk about the peasants working for so little. There were a lot of informers, so they told that he looked like the guy that killed a policeman; they framed him. He was in jail five years and eight months on a frame. The Socialist Party paid for a lawyer's fee; otherwise, they would have killed him. He went through plenty. He was in jail first in our town, then Minsk. I lived across the street from the jail. [I would bring him lunch. They let me because I fixed their watches for free.] I admired him very much; he was an idealist.

Then they changed the law. In Nikolai's time, they didn't [draft] political [prisoners]. But the war was going on, and he told me in a letter they changed the law. So he finished jail and they drafted him right there. It was very, very bad. He was actually fighting in the war in Belorussia. [But one time] he traveled the whole night to come home to see me, and he had to be back the next day. He was so in love with me.

Then the Germans occupied our place. My husband brought soap from Odessa to sell. At the time of the war, you couldn't get a piece of soap. And I used to sell it to the soldiers—fix their watches and sell them soap. I didn't charge them much. They used to come with the Jewish girls: they speak similar language—German and Jewish— so they couldn't talk to the Gentile girls because they couldn't under- stand Russian. I'm telling you, we had a lot of fun. They used to be very nice to the Jewish girls. I fixed up a girlfriend of mine with a German soldier. They weren't Nazis, you understand.

My husband was wounded in the war. It was deep—it penetrated to his bone. A private doctor saved his life. He said, "I wouldn't let you amputate your leg. You will be all right. Time will tell." They put him down for a furlough for three months, so he came home. And he used to make the bandages while I was fixing the watches. My father would say, "My daughter, she's got a good business, she's making a nice living. Why should she marry a cripple?" My father hated him.

My mother liked him very much, but my father used to be so mad. He used to lock me in my room, I shouldn't open the door. He hated him because he didn't go to *shul* with him. My mother—it was her brother's son—my mother was for him. She used to like to talk to him about politics. And I was a rebel. I was fighting and I says, "I love him and I'm gonna marry him. It won't help you." [At the wedding] my father didn't say "*mazel tov*" to my mother-in-law. She didn't talk to him and he didn't talk to her.

I went once to *mikveh*, and then I rebelled. [When I gave birth to my daughter] I had a midwife. We had a wooden bathtub and hot water to give her a bath, and the house was so cold. My father read psalms.[10] I didn't rest much [after childbirth]. On the third day, I was walking and making meals, cleaning the house. We made a swaddle, like a long, long belt for the baby.[11] I turn it around and turn it around and she's like a little bird. You cannot break a finger. I used to feed her *kasheh* and farina.

After the first year, I wanted to get a divorce because I was going through an awful lot, you know; the whole family was on my shoulders. Especially in a small town, and he [my husband] is the big shot from that town, everybody knows who is his wife and who is his father-in-law and who is his mother-in-law. The police station was across the street of my house.

So I said, "Look. You promised me not to participate anymore, not to be that active, you understand." He was very busy. The Bolsheviks made him a big shot. I wanted him to stop. I used to be so tired, and he used to come so late, two, three o'clock in the morning, and not having a key. He used to knock on my window to open the door for him; and I accepted the waking up the family, my father and my mother, so he could go to his meetings. [But finally] I gave him an ultimatum.

I couldn't sacrifice my family. Many times I was thinking of my personal life, my children. I says, "You should choose—either the Party or me." He says, "No. I love you too much to give you up! I wouldn't do it." See over there, for five rubles, you got a divorce from the rabbi. He wouldn't want to give me a divorce.

[But he went anyway to fight] with the Bolsheviks. There was civil war and fighting. Then the bands came, and he heard that we had a *pogrom* in our town. He don't know if I'm alive, if the baby is alive. Denikin or Kolchak or Balachowicz was in our town and they killed a lot of people. The peasants said, "Balachowicz is here; you cannot save yourself."[12]

We escaped. I had a Jewish couple that lived with me, and he had a horse and wagon. And he took me with the baby, with my sister, to hide ourselves at the peasants' in the little villages, I never thought that I'm gonna be alive. My father-in-law was killed: he went to *shul* to pray. A priest hid my mother-in-law. A woman was sitting milking a cow—they came and killed her.

I took all the watches with me. I knew they were going to rob everything in the house. They took even out the windows. When we came back, we found only four walls. The doors they took out. The peasants helped them; they said the Jews were Bolsheviks.

I took the Gentiles watches—that saved us; otherwise, they wouldn't take us in. They were nice but they were afraid for their own lives. Some were afraid the others shouldn't tell that they're hiding Jews in the house. "I'll let you sleep here but the next day, you should leave my house because I'm afraid the others would tell." [They fed us] baked potatoes, tea with saccharin. Then we went further down and further down; we knew the bandits wouldn't be long in power—the Bolsheviks would come back. A couple of weeks we ran, [each night] in different places.

[When my husband came back], he was captured by the bands. The main officer of the post office, a Gentile, I used to fix watches for him, I didn't charge him. Once, they thought that he's against the Bolsheviks, so they arrested him. So I went, and I said, "This man you're taking, this man who had five children and a family, he didn't do anything wrong." And they let him go.

So when they arrested my husband, right away he heard—it's a small town. He came and he says, "[I came] as soon as I saw in the papers what's going on, that your husband is arrested. You don't have to be afraid. I happen to be a friend of the leader of the band. I'll go there and I'll talk to him." And he did. He went there with me, and everybody saw him going with me. They thought that he's going to tell on my husband, on me, but he remembered what I did for him when he was in trouble.

[Then] we heard that the Bolsheviks are coming back, they are near our town. Lucky. The band was going away because the Bolsheviks were not far. [They took my husband], but while the train was going, he jumped out—grass all around, soft, and he was laying down. They would have shot him, but they can't be bothered. They were afraid for their own life.

[Even after this, he continued working for the Bolsheviks.] I was not angry, but he told me that he don't know exactly when they want him to go someplace else, to organize or do some work, so I have to give up my business, my work.

I felt that's my responsibility. My whole family depends on it. My mother is sick, my sister is so young, a little kid. I was like a mother to her, you know. And I would have to go with him and it wasn't stable. He went to Moscow, he worked for the Foreign Department, and he got a room that all the big shots from Nikolai—his ministers —lived there. Maids, I would have, "Everything, darling," mine, but how long until they send him and he's got to go? My father said, "Why didn't they kill him in the war?"

When I wrote him the letter I cannot come, he was very mad. Everybody used to say, "You refused to go? If my husband would call me . . ." I would rather live in my place whether it's cold, or whether it's dusty. I would rather be here than to go there and not know what the next day would bring.

[Meanwhile] another sister came to this country. That's the one that imported us. My sister was so beautiful. [A suitor sent her a ticket.] And she came and she looked at him—he was so ugly. And then she told me that he's forcing her to marry him because he paid for the ticket second class. So I sat down and I wrote her a big letter and I says, "What do you think, you're buying yourself a dress or a coat? No and no. If you have no love for him, if you have no feelings for him, wait until you start working. If you don't love him, don't you dare." She married someone else. They borrowed money to bring us here: me, my husband, my daughter, my mother, my sister, and my brother-in-law's sister. [My father was dead.]

I wasn't sure my husband will be able to go. They will stop him to kill him because he's not free, he's not supposed to go to a capitalist country. He was suffering; he was so disillusioned. He says write to my sister. "I'm ready to go because I can't take it anymore." People were starving. Corrption. When my husband wrote me [that] letter, I was the happiest person in the world. "Write a letter right away to get the visa, the passport." In the middle of the night, two o'clock in the morning, you never knew when they're gonna knock on your door and pick you up and put you to the wall. I was so happy to get him away from there.

[To be able to leave] I sold a lot of things. I sold the place in the synagogue.[13] What do you got? You sell your samovar, some other belongings. We were in Moscow; I had to get the passports by myself because he knew a lot of people from work. My husband was afraid they would kill him, so when I took the papers, he was waiting on a corner for me. He says, "Now for sure, we're going to this country." We went through Danzig, Germany, and Liverpool.

When I got to this country, I used to read in the papers the suffragists in England, what they do.[14] They used to throw tomatoes, rotten apples. I still remember because I used to read *Russka Islova*. This paper was from Kiev. I wasn't just sitting; I used to read. I was really surprised. After all, in the Old Country, in the small towns, the women could bear children without going to school or to college. Figure, all right; she'll meet a man and she'll get married and she will have to bear children; and that's all, that's enough. And I was so sorry that I was born and raised in a small town, that I didn't have the opportunity to learn something better.

[We stayed] at my sister's house. She took us in in four rooms. She used to sleep with her husband and her boy in one three-quarter bed; in the bedroom, I slept with my husband and baby. My mother slept in the kitchen on a folding bed. My younger sister slept in the front room. I lived with them six months. Until they rent me an apartment. At that time, very hard to get an apartment with a child. My sister's husband signed the lease for us. The landlord said, "They are green-horns. Maybe they won't make a living. You better sign the lease." I used to be mad when they used to call me green. I said, "How long does it take not to get green?"

The first week, my husband went to work. He was in the painting business—painting and decorating. He learned that for three years, before he was freed from jail [in Russia]. In jail, he met a man; he liked my husband because he did the writing for him [to get] released from jail. So he happened to be here in this country and he happened to meet that man and he says, "I'll do something for you. I'm in the union." So right away, they took him in in the union. He had that break through this man, through a man who used to steal horses. Here, he was a *macher* in the union.

Right away, I worked in a very big factory. My sister took care of my daughter. I used to make fourteen dollars a week, tie the boxes. I had a watch, so the foreman fired me. He says, "You know, you're telling [workers] the time. You shouldn't tell them" [and distract them].

Then I worked for a watchmaker just a couple weeks. He says, "You tell them this is broken, the mainspring is broken," to get a better price. Teach me all the tricks. He let me go because we moved to a little house in a different neighborhood. I rented to a Jewish couple. They paid me twenty dollars a month. We used to send it to my husband's mother in

Russia. Forty-five dollars the apartment; twenty dollars the room because it was private and steam-heat.[15]

Then I didn't work. I was fortunate because my husband had a good trade. I went to night school; not long enough because I had my boy. He used to cry, "Come home, Mama; come home." He was six years younger than my daughter. I gave it up; I couldn't help it. But my husband helped me. He used to mark articles in the paper. He said, "Stop a little bit the Jewish and read more English." We had a very happy life together because he was at home safe. My life improved. They do a lot of injustices here, too, but still, if you would have been there, you think this is a paradise.

I had an abortion. I didn't want it but I didn't want to have more children. I heard from a cousin of mine a doctor and he charged fifty dollars. One woman came and she had a ring and she said she has no money; he says, "Give me the ring." The doctors are all money-grabbers. I came in and he didn't hurt me at all. He put me out so I didn't know. Then he told me to go home.

In the Depression, my husband lost everything but he used to do the painting on payments. It's better than not to work altogether. So I didn't have to work.

My husband died after Pearl Harbor. He went to bed and didn't get up. Then my daughter insisted I move in with her. She says, "I got a good apartment; I got a good home. I'll make the meals." My friends used to say, "What are you doing, giving up your home?" I says, "Since my husband died, it's no home."

I worked for Montgomery Ward. Watchmakers they had. And they asked me, "How many watches can you produce during the day?" and I said between seven and eight a day. I was very fast. I was the only woman.

Then I worked for Hart, Schaffner and Marx sewing men's crotches. I went to Florida for my vacation, and deep in my mind, I wanted to quit. I came late on purpose. They fired me.

But I wanted to learn and I wanted to see. I wanted to do something. I want to be a productive woman. I didn't believe in staying home and taking care of the kids. So I worked for my sister in her grocery store about two years. I learned how to sell. Then I ran from store to store to knock on doors looking for another job before Christmas, and I got a job by Hillman's Bakery. I fought to get that job. I told them I was ten years younger—it wasn't marked on the face. I was so happy, I couldn't have gotten Social Security otherwise. So I used to eat lunch with the girls, sit and talk; they used to tell me dirty jokes. I enjoyed it very much. I worked part time, but I used to fight [and picket] when we had a strike. My daughter said, "You're a part-time worker, what do you care?" "No. I'm gonna fight: all for one and one for all." And I belonged to the union. Then they wanted to get rid of me because I was older and they could have girls come and work cheaper.

I tried everything. I was fighting for my existence. I'm telling you. I'm going to be eighty-one; I wonder that I live that long. Believe me—I'm thinking of it many times. I must be strong. My grandchildren don't know what I went through.

Rose Soskin

Rose Soskin: The Hungry Child

Rose Soskin's account of her family's struggle for survival in a war-front town in Poland during the First World War is a compelling story of deprivation and suffering, an anti-war testimony which has the power to move as few stories can.

At times, her family had nothing to eat but boiled water and grass. Yet their religious devotion was at least as great as their courage. No one in her family rebelled against the hardships of the war years by rejecting the many religious requirements applying to food. They all still maintain and take pride in their faith, their traditions, and their *kosher* homes. There is always an abundance of food on Mrs. Soskin's table, as though she is still making sure no one will go hungry.

Mrs. Soskin maintains a strong belief in a masterful God in whom she takes comfort. Such a faith undoubtedly sustained her during the long years of fighting and successive occupations while her family was unable to communicate with their father in America.

She is the youngest wife in this book, married to a Polish doctor before she was fourteen and a mother before she was fifteen. When she remarried after a divorce, she was an adult recovered in many ways from the war years and ready for the pleasures a happy marriage could bring. Now, at sixty-nine, she enjoys a hard-won capacity for relaxation and a rediscovered peace.

HONESTLY, it was terrible there.
We never had all this food that is here on this table. That was hunger,
plain hunger. There weren't even potatoes anymore. They didn't have
a good income to live on. They didn't have a chance of raising children
or giving them an education. So that's bitter, that's bitter.

I was born in 1906. We were raised in Semiatycze, Grodnoguberniia.
Originally, it was Poland. Then it became Russia because the Bolsheviks came in, and then the Germans came in and chased out the
Bolsheviks. We had the Germans for four years. They were pretty
nasty, but not as bad as in World War II. I remember. I can close my
eyes and see the whole town. It's such an old town, a friendly town.
Even the *goyim* weren't so mean.

My father was a weaver.[1] He made carpets. There was a factory in
Semiatycze—maybe about ten people worked there, all men. They used
to get paid from the city. They had to roll up their own yarn, and I
used to come into the factory and help him. My mother used to ask me
to go there and help Poppa. Most of the kids used to come and help.
So he would make a few cents more when I would get the thread ready
for him. I was a very young girl. You made [enough of] a living about
to manage. We didn't have luxuries.

We were five children, and we only had one bedroom. I'll never forget
it. We used to sleep on top of the oven. We had an oven for Friday; my
mother used to put in some potatoes and make the oven go all through
the Friday night when we would have wood to make the oven; and
otherwise, it would be cold.[2]

When we used to go to pick wood in the woods, or pick berries, they
wouldn't let us. Because, you see, we were Jews. The *skutsim* used to
throw stones or take a nice long piece of wood and chase us. I still
have one mark from a cane that he was chasing me, and I fell down,
I couldn't run anymore. He just beat me so that my foot was split up

and I was bleeding like a pig. And when I got home, my mother (I'll never forget it), she took a slip and tied it on my foot so the blood shouldn't run so fast.

We had goats. We had our own milk. We had our own gardens too, in back of the house. We didn't have a toilet. We used to have it in the attic, a pail; we used to go to the pail and carry it away at night in the fields.

We had a well. When we used to want to have some fun, we used to turn it up and let it turn down by itself—so many times that the pail would break and we would run away. We would be scared to be caught. All kinds of tricks we used to have.

On the well, in the winter, we used to go skating, for it was very slippery there. We used to put a piece of wood on our shoe, tie it with a string to skate. Break our neck. I still got a mark because one time, I was skating and one of the boys wanted to make a trick, so he put his foot right onto mine, and my piece of wood twisted and I fell on my head.

We all spoke Polish and we were all going to school. We had two schools, a Polish school and a *folkschule*, and we had a Hebrew school for boys. Boys and girls both went to Polish school in the morning. You could attend all three of them, but you had to go to the Polish school; it was a must.

In the Polish school, we had to stand on our knees on Sunday and sing, and we had to cross ourselves, even if we were Jewish girls; otherwise, they wouldn't let us go to the school. We couldn't get an education, unless we do what they want us to do. I don't know; maybe their idea was that everybody was against them, you see? They killed plenty, too. They killed some citizens in the town that were just innocent people. One fellow that used to date my older sister was talking back to the Polacks (that was before the Bolsheviks came in), and they said, "He's a Bolshevik." He was trying to hide, and they killed him. His own parents had to take him to the cemetery on a board. It was a terrible tragedy—just martyrs.

Then the time of war was marching on Poland. They had the front right in the town. We were right near the Wisla and the Bug, the two rivers they were fighting about. The Wisla is the river that separates Poland from Germany. You couldn't go out, the bullets was always going over, you know.

Then the Russians came in. They brought in Russian teachers, and we had to learn the Russian language. And they made us sing in Russian the *Internationale* in school. We had to talk Russian in the street when we got out from school.

We had about three synagogues, but they burned them down. They didn't like the Jewish religion to be kept up. They wanted everybody to go with them, to be Russian. They didn't allow religion in school even.

When the Germans came, we were forced to learn German. We were learning all kinds of German songs. We were young kids; young kids are easier to learn, and to forget, than grownups. Everything was just come and go, you see. Here in the United States, we're doing things in American way; there, we had to do Polish way, we had to do Russian style, we had to do German style, and we were pushed from one school to the other, and from one style to the other. Our education was very hard.

We played jacks with the bullets. We used to go out and pick up those little bullets on the street. My mother used to pull us in by the hair and holler and scream at us, but then the next day, we would do the same thing. We didn't realize some of them could explode, see? We were just kids, you know.

Every day after school, the soldiers used to have a truck right near the school to pick up the kids. We used to go out and work in the woods. We were afraid to say anything because, you know, if you don't want to do what they want you to do, then you'd be in more trouble. I remember they gave us a sharp thing that goes into the tree, and it comes out like honey; but it's not honey, it's not syrup, it's some juice from the white trees. In time of war they needed that. They didn't hurt us, they would just let us do this work for the day and bring us home at night. They would give us cooked chocolate milk and a fresh roll, but my mother said that wasn't *kosher* so we couldn't have it. My mother would explain that it's not the right thing to do, and we wouldn't do anything wrong.

We used to be hungry in school and hungry when we came home from school. It was tough, it was tough quite a few years. Just smelling bread was enough for us. My brother must have been about five years old, and he said he smelled bread and he cried all day. My mother said there is no bread anywheres. Then we found out a neighbor of ours had baked some. So my mother sent me to go and ask if she could spare one slice for my brother. Well, she gave us a slice but she says never again to come or to go through the street with it.

They couldn't go to Russia to bring anything in, you see, and that town was just like cut off from the world. We never had any clothes or shoes enough. When we came here, we were so hungry for food, we always talk about it. My mother used to have to buy a chicken for Saturday to make soup, so she would buy three chickens; she would cook a pot rice and soup and a lot of potatoes and a lot of bread, and pushed in us: eat, eat, eat. When we came in Ellis Island, they put on the tables white bread, so as much as we could eat, we would eat, but we were trying to save whatever was left on the tables for later. We were always afraid we'll be hungry, you know.

For four years, the Germans stayed, and they cleaned out everything in the town. We couldn't get butter, we couldn't get eggs, we couldn't get cheeses, we couldn't get anything, and then they started taking away cows, so it was just impossible to keep alive. Even if there would be anything, we didn't have money to buy. We had trouble with the money: when the Russians came in, it was Kerensky's money; they went out, their money wasn't valued for anything.

All of our life, seems like whatever I can remember, was a lot of hardship, for not only ourselves. Most of the women's husbands were in the United States. My mother was only thirty-three years old when my Pa left, and left her with five children, and my baby brother was only four years old. Pa came here before the war started. He was supposed to be a soldier, one that had to go in front. I remember this like a dream. I remember that my mother was running around to sell all the copperware (we had all kinds of candleholders and copper goods). She tried to sell everything, all her jewelry, to get the money. She had a golden chain with a golden watch; in the Old Country, when they get married, the mother-in-law and the father-in-law give jewelry to the bride. She gave it up—she was always talking about it because it was very dear to her.

She wanted him to go to Galveston because my father had trouble with his eyes; he couldn't go into Ellis Island because they wouldn't let him into this country on account of his *trakhoma*.[3] And so he went to Galveston and Chicago. My mother was supporting us when my father went to this country. She had a business in Semiatycze; we had a store of our own. The stores were in a market. The farmers bring out

Thursdays, chickens; they bring out eggs; they bring out cheese to sell to the people from the town. She had the store till the war started; then she didn't get merchandise. She had to give it up 'cause when you open it and a soldier would come by, he would take all the merchandise away. The stuff that we had was only to sell for farmers. We didn't sell them food; they brought food to us. But [then] too many soldiers were marching all the time; you can't just get through them. The farmers' [goods] would be confiscated, so they wouldn't come out anymore. And then every kind of commercial [enterprise] stopped.

There were no jobs, and almost all of the stores closed up anyway. The people that had stores would put some stuff in the cellar to save some food for their own families. In a time like this, people are just thinking how to survive themselves. They don't worry about the neighbors or about even the relatives.

During the day, we couldn't go out; the war was in our town. It was like the front, you know; they were shooting all through, so nobody went out. [If] we were sticking our nose even through the window, we were scared. Then we were forced to take things that didn't belong to us, so we can eat. We didn't go steal in joy or anything but we would have to go and take some potatoes or turnips just to keep up, just to keep from dying from hunger. We could eat even grass that time, like cows. We were really hungry, desperate for everything that's food. And if you had some goats, you had to keep them in the attic because they'd take them right off of your hands, and they'd kill them. We kept our goats in the attic for five years. I remember that we had to lose them finally. They killed them in our backyard, right outside our house. They cut off their heads and they skinned them and they cooked them.

We used to go to the *dorf* to get some potatoes from the farmers because we didn't have a thing to eat. You can get all you want on the farm—potatoes and milk was pretty tasty those days. We used to almost get caught at night. We went because they would attack my mother for sure, the soldiers. You can't do it all in one day, so we used to sleep over by the *goyim* on the floor, sometimes in a garage. The farmers never hurt anybody.

We were walking through back roads, and still, my sister and I, when we would see from far some soldiers coming, we would lay down in the corner in the fields or in the grass, just flatten out, and wait until they would pass. They didn't stop us, but my sister's friend they attacked. She had a baby, you know; that's how bad it was.

We would bring needles, thread, safety pins, matches; sometimes we used to get some candy to bring there to the farmers. They didn't have money to give us, but we didn't want any money; we wanted potatoes, bread, carrots, turnips, beets, anything. We couldn't even accept salt pork or things like that—it's not *kosher*. Whatever they gave us, we were happy. They take some of our stuff and they bring out something. Some of them didn't let us in the house even. They brought out a chunk of bread, you know, from a big loaf, and put it in our sack. We'd go to the next neighbor, we would knock on their doors and get something. We were not the only ones.

We were right on the front so we were always hiding in the basement, day and night. We didn't know what day it is or what time it is. We just kept saving our lives. Most of the time, we were drinking boiled water, water that we could get out to get. Many times, my mother, she should rest in peace, used to run out at night to the fields for water and potatoes, turnips, carrots, beets. And we were always looking from the basement to the street to see if Mommy's coming because without her, we were just like lost.

And then we couldn't make a fire. The soldiers would march by and they would see smoke coming out the chimney, they would break the door down and come in. One time, I think it was Friday, my mother got some turnips, but we couldn't eat them—they were too hard. So she says she'll just try to cook them a little bit. We couldn't wait until they got soft, but when she tried to cook the turnips, the smoke was coming. And we hear the Polacks; my mother says: "Kids, let's all stay together," and we were all tying up with my mother. All of a sudden, you hear the knock and the door was broken off, and there must have been six or seven [soldiers].

This picture, I can close my eyes or open my eyes. Many times I lay down and I'm thinking of that: it was such a funny way, how they were so angry, and they were so mean when they were outside; they said when they find any Jewish people, they'll cut their throats like you'll kill in the stockyards. Life made them so aggravated: they didn't sleep enough, their life didn't mean anything. The soldiers were not particularly after anybody, but they were hungry. They'd fight for food. But when they came in, they all started laughing instead of being mean, you see; they saw we were all holding onto my mother all around her and my mother wasn't a bad-looking woman. We didn't understand what it means to be attacked, or to be raped. Those things we were too young to [know], and we never got explained like in this country. But my mother understood, and she was afraid that they'd come in and God forbid they should do something like that to her. So she wouldn't even comb her hair. She would look bad so she wouldn't be attractive on the top of everything.

So we gave them water, and we gave them the turnips; we were grabbing pieces ourselves. We were all very hungry.

When the Germans gave up, ammunition, everything they threw down. They were hitchhiking on the road. They put them in jail. And they were dying, hundreds of them. They used to bring them into the church from the fields, from the front. They don't care where they throw them and nobody can say anything. They used to bring them laying one on the other, some of them were even still breathing; and then they used to bury so many in piles.

It was something I think I could write about ten books and never get through with it because that's terrible, you know. A war is a funny thing, see; there are so many bad things happening that you just can't imagine that could ever happen in your life. You can live through your whole life, you could never go through the experience that people go through when they live through a war, in a town especially that the war is right on.

When the war began, my father went to this country. We didn't hear from him for over four years. He couldn't get through with any mail because for four years we were cut off. After it quieted down and the immigration opened up, some of the American husbands sent money to their wives with letters to find out if they were still alive because in the town where we were, they didn't expect many to be alive. We were just like lost there, and my mother used to cry a lot because she worried that Pa maybe has got somebody else here. You know, he was a young man. He came here, he was thirty-eight years old. So she was worried, jealous; I don't know.

Then an American fellow was sent from a bank in Chicago by HIAS to investigate if there are many women that the husbands are in America and the women are still in Poland.[4] He brought a postal card from my father. My father didn't save much money; he wasn't the type to worry about what's going to be. When he came in this country, he became a *shammes* in the *shul*—my father was very highly educated in Hebrew.

[The HIAS man] had to make a passport to send us immigration papers. He had to know the exact date when we were born. Here when a child is born, you get a birth certificate from the hospital the first day with the date and everything. There when a child is born, you don't have a birth certificate. You remember where you used to live and how long you stayed there. My mother had a hard time to recollect from the five children the exact date of birth, and it was too many things went through her mind by the time of war.

While we waited for the papers, I got married. He was a doctor, a graduate of Heidelberg University, practicing in our town. I was very young, thirteen and a half years old. He was thirty-five. He fell in love with me when he came back from university. In the Old Country, when a doctor wants to marry you, you marry. It was mostly my mother's idea. I was too young to fight. She said it would be the best thing. I wouldn't say no because she said in this country, I'll have to get married to a shoemaker, which would not be in our family nice. My girlfriends were all jealous of me because I was marrying a doctor. On top of that, he was a very rich boy. I was the first married in our family.[5]

In the Old Country, in the first year of marriage, you lived with the parents of the bride—that goes in the dowry.[6] I didn't know nothing. I was enjoying the life of being together with a man. He wanted to marry me and some would think maybe he was hungry for a woman. He loved me, I think; I wouldn't say he didn't, and I loved him very much, too; but I didn't know what love means. We loved our parents and we loved our brothers and sisters. I was too young. Girls should never get married that young. Not sooner than twenty-one because they don't know what they want to do and what they are, what life is all about.

In nine months, I had a boy delivered by a midwife. We had a *bris* and a *pidyon haben*. That means when the first boy in the family is born, you make a sort of celebration.

My father's brother sent a thousand dollars to a bank in Warsaw for us to come to the United States, and he sent us ship cards, one-way trip tickets. We went down to Warsaw; my husband Josef was with us. It was 1921, but we delayed for two years. We were supposed to be shipped with a group to the United States, but we were stopped on account of my oldest brother. He had scarlet fever, and his hair didn't grow right. So my mother had to go with him every day for electrical treatments to make the hair grow back. It took a long time.

We had to live in Warsaw for two years. We had to live very economically to stretch the money that we got from America for two years —five people, you know. We used to eat only in the midday, lunch, and then we made it [until] the next day. We couldn't afford three meals in a day.

We stayed in a boarding house because we couldn't stay with my rich uncle [my mother's brother]. We were too big a family. But he used to bring us some food there, take me to a show. And then they had electric lights in Warsaw. Such trolleys they had. We had stones and mud most of the time in our town, and the sidewalks were already a luxury to see. We used to sit around and wait till the next day; that's all you could do there.

Before we were shipped from Warsaw, we didn't have any money left, and my father's brother had to send us more—seven hundred dollars, big amount. We had to have some money to get started, to buy things for the kids—shoes, and the clothes were all worn out. We came in 1923 with the *Mauretania*.

My father was here, and my father's brother. We were three sisters and two brothers and my mother when we got to this country. My husband stayed in Warsaw for a while.

We lived on the West Side.[7] When you go to the butcher shop, you'd speak Yiddish. And when you go to an American show, you speak English. We had five rooms with two bedrooms, a front room with a big mirror on the side.

We all started working right away. I started to work in a tailor shop, men's clothes, just when I came, maybe three or four days. A *landsman* of ours, from the Amalgamated Union, took me down to give me a job.[8] You see, my mother called him to try to get a job for me and my younger sister.

Right away, I went to evening school. Maybe I was about two weeks in this country. My mother was taking care of the baby; then she herself started going to learn English.

My mother got a diploma, and I got a diploma at the same time. My sister, too. Then I went to high school for two years, but then they didn't let in immigrants, so we couldn't get any more public school education. I went to a private school because I was working, and I always thought that I have a chance to get out from the foreign accent.

I didn't know how to go to work at the tailor shop. I says to my Pa,

"Would you please mark down the address where the place is in case I get lost or don't know where to get off the bus?" He says, "I don't have to mark. You go as far as North Avenue. There is a bank that sticks out and you get off by the bank." Well, I got on the bus. I dozed off a little, and I kept opening my eyes and looking for that bank. I didn't see the bank. I went back to sleep; I figured I'm still early. It's hard to imagine how far you are, you know, when you sleep. So I wake up; I look. I'm in a barn, you know; it's just nothing but cars standing there, out of the way, and a fellow comes and knocks on the back. And I didn't know what he was talking —I didn't know one word English— so I just turned around, and I took my lunch in my hand and my pocketbook and I didn't know what to say. But he saw that I must have been a greenhorn, and he says, "You Polska?" So I says to him in Polish there a few words, so he [tells me how to go]. They moved the bank that morning. So when I got to the shop about five hours [late], I felt so embarrassed.

There were about four hundred people, mostly men, in that tailor shop. A five-story building; it was nice. People were nice to me. Some were Jewish; mostly Greeks and Italians. We got along. It was a union place.

In the beginning, I used to get fifteen dollars a week for floor worker. I was marking lapels for the coats. Then when you get to do a different job that belongs to the union, you have to belong to the union. [After I joined], I was working on a serging machine, zigzag; it's a machine with a double needle. You sew the seams for the sack coats before they are sewed by the operator; they have to be stitched together that they shouldn't rip. I used to sew about four hundred an hour. You got to go real fast because if you don't, you never make your bonus [for exceeding the quota]. Instead of fifteen, I used to make seventy-five dollars a week. I used to be very fast, and even those men that used to work in the shop (some tailors) used to come around with the envelope, it used to be cash, and they used to say, "Roseleh, how much?" I was ashamed to show because they jealous, you see.

When we first came in this country, the beginning of our Chicago life, we used to go Saturday after work to the beach.[9] I remember that there used to be swings on the sand. There was a Polish *shiksa* on the swing, and she was on for a long time, so when she came down lower a little, I says, "Miss, when are you getting off the swing?" She says, "You're a dirty Jew. Why don't you go to the bank on Saturday and deposit your money? I'm not getting off the swing." I say, "What do you mean, 'dirty Jew'? Explain, and I'll let you down. Otherwise I'll pull you down by your hair." I was strong and I was excited. I still had that European life in me a little, you know—the blood I brought with me. So she tried to get up higher back with the swing and to ignore that I said she's been too long on the swing and has to give somebody else a turn. Well, she had long hair. I pulled her down by the hair, and we were fighting in the sand for quite a nice long time. But she got some kind of a spasms and some white foam was coming from her mouth, you know; but I digged her in the sand so bad until her hair was more on my hand than on her head. And I says, "You better take it back that you said dirty Jew; take it back—otherwise I'll never let you out of my hand." Well, she says, "I'm sorry, I'm sorry, I'm sorry"; she was screaming. I wouldn't let her get away with it. I would kill her if she wouldn't take back her words. There's no such thing as calling somebody names like this, especially in a free country.

We had to work on Saturday, though we're not supposed to.[10] We used to be real good when we first came here, but we looked around. We have to make a living, you know, and we couldn't keep a job that we don't keep the five and a half days a week.

But we stayed very religious. In the house, we were pretty firm. When we went out, I didn't eat *trayf*. We never made a light on Friday; we never touched a fire. We never could go against my father especially. We would honor our parents; we still all keep *kosher* house. I wouldn't eat *trayf* because it would just make me sick. When I buy the *kosher* meat, I still *kosher* it—salt and soak it. I do these things for my soul to feel good, that's all. My children, when they come to my house, they know they're going to have a kosher dinner with all the trimmings. But there are some things I don't keep up. On Sabbath, I answer my phone. I am, I would say, a modern Jew.

Well, all this time we were working and gave Mother the money for the rent—my father never made enough. My father sent papers for Josef, my husband, to come and he did, two years after I entered this country. We lived with my mother.

When Poppa passed away, my mother decided to open up a fruit store, and she did pretty good. She liked to be independent. The only thing, she was homesick for her family. She used to talk about her family; she was hoping some day that she could get together with them. I really don't know what happened to all of them. Many times I'm wondering. We went to this country and left everything behind and that's it. You know, I would never want to go back there either. I'm not lonely for anything that I left behind, but she missed them so we used to go to the Semiatycze *verein*.[11]

Then I divorced my husband. He worked at the hospital; there was a nurse working with him and he was a very handsome guy. She was driving a car, and she used to take him to work, so he always used to kiss her goodnight in the car. I was so jealous, and I got modernistic in this country. I understood a little bit my way, so I gave him a divorce. I wanted a Jewish divorce. Cost me five hundred bucks about.

When I met my [second] husband, I started to realize life. He was the electrical engineer in the basement of the Jewish People's Institute.[12] I used to dance with my friends on the roof garden on Sunday, and then go down in the basement and watch them play pool. There used to be a cafeteria in the basement. I went once for coffee and he was sitting there; we start talking, and he wouldn't let me go, that's all there is to it. I went out with him for about a year. We had a nice wedding. My husband too was very observant, so to *mikveh* I went every month. My mother used to take me on Thursday night. I couldn't sleep with him any other way. We were very happy for thirty-five years. Then he had a heart attack and died. Nothing we can do then.

My son was dead, too. He had been married to a Gentile girl. He was killed in the Luxembourg invasion and he never came back. They brought him back with his box, and they never let me see, so we have to believe that he's in there, that there's no mistake on top of everything which I always was hoping that it was a mistake. It's twenty-eight years have passed; proves you have to believe in God, that it was meant that way, that's all there is to it. If not for believing in God, that it's God's will, then I guess we would go crazy.

It's twelve years that I am living by myself and keep up my own style of life. I'm old and I don't feel too good. It's nothing anybody can do. When you're alone, you're alone. [If] you live with children, you bring sin on [them because] you give them a chance to fight their parents. I had chances to be married again, but I wouldn't want to bother. I don't know. I enjoy my family, my life, and that's it, just living and enjoying. Life is experience, is your teacher. You see, you can't tell children or anybody to be like I was thirty years ago. I feel it's a modern life now.

PART TWO

How They Came . . . The Passage to America

I had dreamed of free schools, free colleges, where I could learn to give out my innermost thoughts and feelings to the world. But no sooner did I come off the ship than hunger drove me to the sweat-shop, to become a "hand"—not a brain—not a soul—not a spirit—but just a "hand"—cramped, deadened into a part of a machine—a hand fit only to grasp, not to give.

—Anzia Yezierska, *Children of Loneliness*

Pearl Moscowitz: The Child Immigrant

Pearl Moscowitz's story illustrates the process of immigration and helps us to realize that it did not involve just the purchase of a ticket and the trip to America.

Immigration meant a momentous decision to leave the familiar for the questionable comfort of a strange country. It involved the hazardous risk—both at the point of departure and at the point of entry—of being turned back with nowhere to go and nothing to live on. An immigrant was a gambler playing with long odds: one had to gather sufficient funds to buy tickets, sell or dispose of possessions that could not be taken, cross the border to get out of the country (legally or illegally), fulfill changing legal and health requirements—often against the backdrop of wars and revolution. Finally, immigration was a process that very often separated families forever, a real and terrifying possibility for Mrs. Moscowitz.

Mrs. Moscowitz was one of eleven children in a family which left rural farm life in Russia in 1914 to come to rural farm life in America. She is a woman who has successfully negotiated migration from the Old World to the New and from farm life to city life in both Russia and America. At eleven, as a child immigrant, she faced adventures and pressures with which few modern American middle-class children, or adults, could cope.

Note: "Pearl Moscowitz" is a pseudonym.

MY FOLKS IN EUROPE, in Russia that is, used to be on what they call an *imenie*—that's a farm. They rented it under a Gentile name because Jews were not allowed to rent land there. For years, my father maintained a nice livelihood. We were eleven children—he provided for us.

My mother's father was called a doctor but he was a *feltsher*—not a genuine doctor, but he can give certain prescriptions for certain things. He had about five, six children and they kept dying. He couldn't [prevent it], although he was himself a medical man. So when my mother became thirteen years old, my grandfather thought maybe he'll change luck. He'll engage her to somebody and maybe that will hold her alive. He knew she was too young to get married, but my grandfather was a rich man. My father's parents weren't, so he says to him, "Look, I'll send you to school. You'll become engaged to my daughter, but I don't want her to get married now because she's too young. Don't worry, you just continue going to school."[1] So that's what he did.

When my mother became fourteen (he was eighteen), she got married to my father; and when she was fifteen, she became a mother. Money was no object. He could have been a *rabbi* if he wanted to, but he never cared for that; he knew the whole history of the *Torah* and everything pertaining to that. Very good knowledge. My father was a brilliant man but he wasn't a man that could make a livelihood. So my grandfather said, "Now it's time for you to stop school, and I'll put you to work," and that's when he started putting him [on the farm]. He's the one who started him off.

Naturally, we had a different life here than my parents had in Russia. In Russia, my parents didn't know anything but work and keeping the farm. There was no excitement, no theaters; and then when we lived in Pinsk, that was the same thing too.

[On the estate,] the peasants would come during the summer to rake the hay and cut the wheat. They had to do it by hand. Women and men would all come out. There would be about twenty-five to fifty people coming out into the morning to do the work. They lived in a little village. They would get twenty-five cents a day for working; and they used to sing those Russian songs. What impressed me as a child—when they used to go home before sunset, the sun was just setting and they'd put their rakes on their shoulders and they would sing those sweetest songs. To me, that was music and they were so happy.

We had maybe a hundred cows there. We used to have about four or five milkers and they would milk by hand. And all the people would come and buy those [cattle and dairy] things. Potatoes and wheat and rye—that's what our livelihood was from. My father sold what he grew to people that had stores or people that sold it to the peasants who needed those things. [He was] an in-between man. And in the wintertime, they used to thresh the wheat and rye. We had a great big barn where they were doing that. And they used to walk from their *dorf* about a mile barefooted on the ice in the wintertime, and they never complained. For lunch, they'd bring some hot soup and a piece of heavy bread. White bread they had only for Easter.

It's unbelievable, the life they lived there; everyone had so many acres of land where they used to raise their own potatoes. They never had a floor in the house, just the earth. And they had a big oven, you'd cook in it and on top they would get the heat and they would sleep on top of that oven in order to keep warm for the winter.

Oh, you should see what my mother used to bake for Friday—the *challehs*, and the *gefilte fish*. I was always a very poor sleeper, so my mother used to sneak out of bed on Friday morning because she had so much baking to do, and quietly she'd go in the kitchen, start preparing everything; but I always heard her, and right away, I'd come in and she'd say, "Oh oh, there she comes." But I couldn't sleep, and I tried to help her, but I was a youngster to begin with.

[Since] my father had the farm under a Gentile's name, of course he used to pay a lot of bribes. See, we knew we were treading on thin ice. We were already told to [leave]; my father was still hoping, he was still paying graft. But it came a time when they refused to accept it; and at that time, one of my little sisters was very ill and Father and Mother took off to Pinsk to see a doctor for the child. We were told that we had to get out of the *imenie*, so the police came, and we begged them to give us a chance to stay another day or so until the parents would come back, but they refused to do that. So, they used to have what they call a *furgon*—a big wagon. We hitched up horses to it, and they took all our beddings and things like that, took all us children (there was quite a big family at that time because we were all still home), and they piled us in this wagon and took us to Pinsk, eight miles from where we were, and we told them where my folks were. A cousin took us in; they went and found an apartment and we moved the family into there. We never went back because we didn't want this experience again.

My father originally wanted to go to America long before, but Mother didn't like it because she had conveniences there—she had a maid—and she felt if she comes to America with a big family, it would be a hardship on her. I had seven brothers and we were four sisters, so when my brothers started to grow up and had to go to the army and they wouldn't let us make a livelihood over there, my father put his foot down and says, "No more Russia. We are going to America." But it took several years before we started off. You couldn't blame my father. He hated Russia.

When the time came for my oldest brother to be ready for the army, my father manipulated. He sent my oldest brother to America, where he had a friend, and he took my younger brother and he substituted for him; although he was only about a year and a half younger, he was little for his age. If they ever caught my father, he was the biggest criminal; he could have gone for the rest of his life to jail. He was a daredevil, my father was, and a bright *yeshiva bucher*. Well, when my oldest brother got his discharge papers, on my other brother's name, that's when he came back to Russia.

[When] we started to go to America, we had three older brothers already in America. My father sent them off first because he wanted them to kind of establish themselves and see what America was like. So then the rest of the family was to follow. He made the passport and was positive that everybody will [pass] that examination of the eyes. It was maybe a month or two before [leaving] that we went to have our eyes examined. They wouldn't let you in unless your eyes were perfect.

There's such thing they used to call *trakhoma*.[2] It so happened out of all the children and my father and mother, everybody was fine; but when it came to me, I had trouble. My father, mother, eleven children, nobody had it but me. We were always together, slept on the same pillow, used the same towel. It was a very catchy thing yet nobody had it. The doctor says you can take her but they won't pass her through.

[Before my parents left, they tried to cure me.] It was really hardship because I went to one Russian doctor in Pinsk. The doctor was just like a murderer. The first thing he did was perform like a surgery. While we were in the office with my mother, there was screaming and yelling—you know how a child that age is worried about it. He examined me and said I have that *trakhoma* and I said, "Doctor, will I have difficulty like the child before me?" He said, "Yes, you have to have the same thing." Well, right then and there I said, "No. I'm not going to do it." But he had a Polish peasant there, and he and my father were holding me on a couch. The doctor used like little tweezers around the top of the eye. He just squeezed out puss. It was very, very painful. And I was just screaming my head off because the pain was so severe.

After that was done, I had to go home and stay in bed for three days with ice packs. Then I went back to him to look it over. They used to cure you with a styptic pencil that was very strong. He would open my lid and just press it with that and he used to put that on. Well, that was even worse than when the surgery was performed because it was very strong like acid, and it was burning for hours. It was so painful it was unbelievable.

Well, anyway, finally we took off. When we came to the border, they stopped me. They said I wasn't cured and they sent me back. It so happened that my folks had to go because their passport was due. Everything was sold and they had to get out. A sister and sister-in-law of mine were still in Russia, so my mother took me [back] to another doctor, a cousin, and she left me there with him.

So I remained in Russia for about eleven months without my parents. I remained with my cousin about six or eight weeks. He was a doctor, but he was a religious fanatic. You didn't dare comb your hair on *Shabbes*. When he got through, he said, "Well, I done all I could for you. Now go back to your sister and make arrangements and go to America. Now remember, don't eat *trayf* when you go."

Well, we thought I was cured. They sent me back to my sister in Luninec. I was staying by her, and of course, I was very lonesome. But I didn't let myself feel that there's no hopes. [Still] I wouldn't sleep nights, and I'd scream in my sleep; I was very unhappy. So one day, I says to my sister I want to go back to the place where I lived. I felt if I go back there, I wouldn't have that depressing feeling. And she says, "You'll never feel any different because the folks are not there." But I used to cry so much and finally she consented. She wrote a letter to my sister-in-law in Pinsk. So I came there. The next morning, I got up and I went to that place where we used to live. You know, I get chills when I think of it now. I mean, I came up to that door and I could not walk into that house. I felt no, they're not there. And I never walked in.

So my sister in Luninec made arrangements, and my sister-in-law was all ready to leave with her two small children. I was going to travel with her. And we went to Germany. They also examined my eyes there and passed me on. From there, they didn't stop me. I came to Antwerp for three or four days, and then our ship was there. My sister-in-law and her children were fine, and they put me to a side. They said that my eyes are not well and I cannot pass the test and I cannot go to America.

So they return us back to the hotel where we were staying, so there was another party that was staying there who had the same difficulty. And that party told my sister-in-law, "Please, if you have any way of sending her back to Russia, let her go back there because I'm here a year so far, I don't see daylight. It seems like it's a lost cause being treated in Antwerp." And of course, it could have been a lost cause because they couldn't cure it. So then my sister-in-law—I went as a minor with her—had to change my age to become a big girl and send me back because she couldn't send me alone [otherwise]. So I had to become of age and I passed at that time for about sixteen.

I went back to my sister in Luninec. We waited till after the [fall] holidays and then we went to Bialystok, where there was a very fine doctor, well-known for eyes. At that time, [doctors] didn't run into high money [and] my father was not a pauper. My luck always followed me: the doctor was out of town, but his nephew was there. And he's examining me and of course my sister was there, so he said to her that the doctor was very busy, he couldn't take me until about five or six days after he arrives (he was arriving tomorrow).

So she turns around and says, "Doctor, I left a baby at home and I have to get back to the baby." So you know, he fell in love with my sister, and I was accepted.

Before we went to him, we went to another doctor that someone said was good. That doctor said the same thing: I cannot go because my eyes are not healed perfect and he didn't ever think that I could travel to America. My sister started crying and I started crying, and you know those people that are in that business—right away, somebody come up, a man comes up, speaks Jewish. He says, "What are you crying for?" Well, he knew what we were crying for. So my sister tells him that my parents are gone and I have this trouble. "Don't worry about it," he says. "There's a way of getting her there." So of course, immediately she questioned him. "Oh, it'll cost you money, but you can get her there. But you must continue healing as far as you can heal."

Then we went to the other doctor that we really wanted, and we explained the situation. He said, "She needs more curing, it's not completed, but," he says, "she will never be able to go to America because there's always a sign that she has had it and they won't permit it."

So my sister says, "What do I do now?" She tells him about this agent [who] said that he can do it; and he says, "Be sure you find a way that he don't take your money and forget about everything. I work through a *rabbi* here. We will negotiate through this *rabbi*." And he gave us the address. Of course, my sister investigated the *rabbi* because anybody can say he was a *rabbi*. But he was well-known, and they said he was a very honest man.

So my sister finally consented and said I'll stay and continue treatments. So I said, "If I never go to America, if I never see my parents, I'm not going through this." The doctor was a little Jewish man, a very brilliant man, such a dear man, and he comes up to me and takes me around and says, "Listen child, I promise you that it won't hurt like that. I don't perform it like that other doctor done. He did both eyes; I will do only one eye at a time, and on my honor, as God is my witness—" he was just like a father—he says, "I will not hurt you." I says no and he walked out of there, and my sister says, "Make me an appointment for tomorrow and she's coming." Well, that night, all night long, I was crying and I kept saying I'm not going. She said, "Look, Pearl. You've got to go to America; your parents are there."

So anyway, I did go into that hospital there. I was screaming, but I really mean screaming. So the doctor slapped me on the face. He gave me like a Novocain and I really quieted down. I didn't feel a thing.

He did one eye and bandaged it up properly. I didn't have to put ice on it. When the anesthetic went out, it was painful, but it was bearable. About a week later, he did the other eye. It was really an experience in my life, and I went through all by myself. And then he said, "Well, now this is out of my hands. You're cured as far as I'm concerned."

[During all this,] I stayed in a rooming house because my sister had to go back to her child. I thought my mother used to cook the best chopped fish in the world. So one night, we sit down to eat and I take a taste of the fish and I said, "My God, it's not my mother's fish." Of course, it brought back all those memories from my mother. And I was very much attached to her. How I ever got along without her is beyond me.

So then we started getting ready for going. But he [the agent] did not get the money [right away]. He said to me, "Forget my name. You are going to get there safe and sound to your folks." He knew he could not get the money until I arrived.

We left from Bialystok. People living by the border had passes to go into Germany and come back. He happened to know somebody who had this privilege. So it was arranged that he would take me as his daughter. I remember the town we had to go to from Germany. So when we came there, everything was fine and we were supposed to go twelve o'clock at night, the later the better. Evidently, somebody snitched, because a man came up and started questioning me and we had to get off the train. He [the agent] still didn't tell the truth; he told him I had acne on my face and that I'm his daughter and he's taking me there for that purpose. But they wouldn't let us go.

So we were taken to a town; it was miles and miles and it was very cold. We had a policeman with us that took us there, besides the driver.

Finally, we reached the place and they put us in jail. It happened to be on a Friday night, and it was very cold in that cell; and you know, the people around (somehow things pass around fast) found out that a Jewish family is being held here, and you should see the fish and the soup and the chicken. There are wonderful people in this world.

So the next morning, we had to appear before whatever the title was. So my agent said to me, "Do not tell the truth." So the same officer that was with us said, "Tell them the truth when you go in there." But I figured I can't trust him, I got to trust the agent that was with me. So finally, the agent says to me, "Tell them the truth."

We were released. We had contact with other people, friends of his, so we went to those people to wait until a train would come to take me back to Bialystok. But the train went—we were too late. Meanwhile, he arranged an okay to go to Germany. So we were lucky that we didn't get on the train [to Bialystok] because if we did, we could not have gone to Germany [and from there to the United States].

The following day, we went through, and I was sitting there—the same thing: "It's your daughter?" "Yes"—and this was it. And from there on is how I came to America. There on, I was all by myself [eleven years old]. I had to even lie I was of age [sixteen] because they wouldn't let me in at my age.

It's funny; the children in Russia are a little more advanced—they're not babies like they are here. But I guess maybe because we were a bigger family, we had to be on our own. We couldn't depend on any-body waiting on us or handing us anything. I may be a coward in some things, but I'm not afraid. If I have to do it, I'm going to do it. From there on, it was fine; I had no trouble at all.

I went through Bremen, and then Hamburg, Germany. I had the papers. The agent over there had it all fixed for me that I could go ahead and have no interference. I wasn't stopped.

Then when I got on that ship, it was eighteen days. When we were on the ship, I remember that some people took very ill right away. I was naturally with the female cabin. We were quite a few in a cabin, about twelve or fourteen women. There were a lot of Jewish people and also Russian. I didn't make acquaintances with anybody because I really and truly didn't know if they were traveling under the same conditions. I just wanted to avoid telling anybody any stories because I knew I was going under false travel.

Everybody told me to be sure to take the top bunk because, you know, people get so seasick, be sure it doesn't come on me. We weren't served food by a table. We were given pails for soups, meats, and desserts. I'm a good sailor; I was never seasick or anything, and every-body used to be so envious of me. So I would get up in the morning for breakfast, and I would go to the kitchen and I would take those pails, and as long as I belong to that cabin, they gave me whatever amounted to for that cabin. But half a dozen or more were sick; they wouldn't even come near the table. They used to get sick seeing me sit down and eat. They wouldn't take anything.

Before it was real rough, the sailor used to come in the morning and say, "Everybody out on deck." Well, you didn't have to coax me twice. I was always out there 'cause I always loved fresh air. We used to stand there and see the seals [porpoises] jumping.

It wasn't the best boat and they were selling in between meals like a hamburger, and naturally it wasn't *kosher*. I didn't mind. I had the money; I bought it. So a Jewish man sits near me; he says in Jewish I didn't arrive yet in this country and I'm already turning to be a *goy*. The people that were strictly *kosher* they used to send off with baskets. They'd stretch it so it lasted. They were really starving. I was never a religious person, but my folks in Russia were strict. When they came here, the times changed them.

We arrived in Baltimore. They have people that take care of travelers. They put me on a train to Chicago, and on the train, I sent a telegram to my parents. My parents did not know whether I was coming or what; they couldn't get any information. Well, they didn't send all the telegrams. Mine didn't go. And then when I got off at the station, I look around, look around, see that nobody's there, and naturally my heart is sunk.

Then these people that supervised foreigners came up to me and said, "Do you see anybody that you know?" I says, "No. Nobody came." She says, "Well, we'll have to take you." It was 1914. So they took me there in a carriage, and it was on a Sunday night and it was kind of late already. Everybody was at home. They knocked on the door, and I hear my mother, "Oh, I'll bet it's a telegram from Pearl"; and when my brother opened the door and I came in—well, you have no idea the reaction of that family.

I was maybe about a week or two the most in Chicago, and then we went to the farm in Michigan. It must have been around January or so because it was very, very cold. My father didn't have a profession to make a livelihood. In the year that he was here [Chicago], he thought he'll go back on a farm. He came with money and he bought it through [an agency] in Chicago.[3] He couldn't do anything else, and there were five young children to be supported. The others were grown and they were already working. He said, "In Russia, I had peasants working for me; we would become peasants here. But my children had a roof over their head and we'll try to make the best of it." There [in Russia], that was such a big place, my father couldn't walk to see if everything was taken care of. He had to get on a horse. Here we had a nice farm, too. It was one hundred twenty acres—used to be a big resort place—but no comparison. Here we had to go ourselves to plant and pick. The money we made was from the small berries. We would take it to the little town and from there [it would go] to Chicago. We raised strawberries, raspberries, cucumbers, eggs. We had an orchard. The only thing we had to buy was flour for bread. My father was a good businessman, but we struggled.

We used to vote on schools, whether eight months or nine months because the children had to get out from school and help their parents on the farm. If we didn't work, then nothing was done. I used to help pick berries and cucumbers, do regular farm work. My father was considered a rich farmer. He always took things that he knew he could make money on. W couldn't afford to have labor. Just the kids there helped, and my brothers would come up [from Chicago]. Then for the fall, they would go back to the city and find themselves jobs. But of course, when my brothers and sisters went to work, they helped us, sending money to maintain the farm. Whatever they could spare.

After we went on the farm, it was impossible to keep *kosher*. We couldn't get any meat. So the children wanted food, so my parents started to buy *trayf*. My father said, "If we can't go over, we have to go under and stop buying *kosher* meats." Otherwise, we [would have] no meat of any kind. [But we'd still celebrate the holidays.] We'd get a *Torah* and [people] would congregate at our house. There were maybe seven or eight Jewish farmers.

Then in fall, I went to school. I couldn't read or write English, but my arithmetic, my other things I could, so it didn't take me long to graduate grammar school.

The town, Covert, had a bigger school, but we had, just right on the corner where our land was, a school there. We had one teacher who taught everything: first grade up to the eighth grade. She would take one class, put them in front of her, and she'd give them so much time; and then she'd call the other class. She managed all; there weren't too many students there—maybe about twenty-five.

And there were mischievous boys. We had stoves to heat the place and when they decided that they didn't want school no more for the day, they'd knock down the chimney, and the teacher would have to dismiss the school.

We were the only Jews. This is something too. That school had a black. This girl was the finest girl in school as far as I was concerned. She was so nice in every way. In Russia, we never saw black people. As a child, when I saw what they were doing to the blacks, I couldn't take it. We were never taught hatred in our home.

I wanted to go on to high school, but my folks couldn't send me. I didn't have enough clothes to wear, shoes to go, so I was embarrassed. I said I wasn't going to go; instead, I'm going to work. The fact is that my folks could not afford to send me. When we graduated, we had to take an exam, and if they found that you passed the test, you got your diploma. Some of the students [who went to graduation in Lansing] came back and said that they said a student from Russia graduated very early and she made her eighth grade. After I heard that, I felt kind of bad. I couldn't go there, but there was no choice.

It's really a life when you reminisce, although I never complained. But my family didn't like it. My brothers and sisters hated the farm; they were wishing we'd sell. I kind of liked the idea of selling, too, but I wasn't bitter. [Finally] they sold the farm and came to Chicago. My father did nothing. It was whatever the children earned they brought it home and this was it. My parents accepted their fate, and whatever they could do, that was it. As I said, my mother never wanted to come to this country. But there was no choice; she never really complained. She just made the best of it and so did my father. We were a family that kind of stuck together and tried to help one another. We didn't have what millionaires have, but really we were a very happy family.

Well, I met my husband there on the farm. It's like a story that you don't believe it could be true. He and his boyfriend were coming out to somebody else's. That night, we had a very big storm, and the lightning struck their house and it burned down. They had no place to go. We had a big home, so when that happened, naturally my folks opened the door for them and told them to come and stay with us until things get straightened out. We married in 1922.

At my age when I got married, there was no such thing as men doing housework. There was no such thing as fifty-fifty. The wife did her share and the man went out to work and provided. So I knew what I was getting into when I got married. I knew I wasn't getting married to a millionaire. I always made the best of that. If you want to make a go of marriage, you have to give a lot and take a lot.

I did work. And then when my children were born, I stopped. My children were first. After they got bigger, I went to work again. I enjoyed my work. Especially when I started working at [Marshall] Field's. Field's was *the* store.

No, I didn't accomplish what I wanted. Because I wanted an education. I took it the way it is and that's the way it's going to be.

Katya Govsky: Getting Here the Hard Way

Sophisticated and well-educated, Katya Govsky was the middle daughter of a privileged family who lived in one of the major cities in Russia. Her grandparents were wealthy. Her father, a clever and resourceful businessman, earned the family a place in the Jewish elite of their city. Her mother was an intellectual, a university lecturer, and a strong model for her children. Mrs. Govsky's identity seems to have been shaped partly in reaction and partly in conformity to her mother.

Although Mrs. Govsky's life began in great comfort, it eventually became one of struggle and danger. Even though her family was part of the upper class, because they were Jews, life was not easy. There were annual *pogroms* even before the Revolution and the civil war that followed. When the family finally decided on emigration, their trek out of Russia proved to be long and dangerous. Once safely outside Russia, the family was delayed six years in France where they waited for the opening of the newly legislated American quota.

In France, both Mrs. Govsky and her older sister attended the Sorbonne. While her sister was able to finish her medical degree, Mrs. Govsky left France before she could complete her studies. She carries this disappointment with her to this day. One only wishes she would see the extent of her accomplishments as clearly as others do.

Note: "Katya Govsky" is a pseudonym.

IN RUSSIA, all of our relatives were rich; they didn't live without maids; they were always dressed beautifully, and they belonged to clubs. They felt to knit and crochet was secondary—that's for a woman who sits home. We had to go to school. That was not the same class of women like they have here [on] the West Side, who knew how to have children and work in the house, and that was a woman. My mother thought that was not for her children.

When I came, to associate with tailors and shoemakers was a disgrace.[1] [Now] I am so much improved; I feel that I acquired so much more knowledge by knowing people with less education. They had a heart and soul and compassion, which is more important than education. I would be a saleslady, a scrubwoman, and that wouldn't disgrace me. To knit, to cook, to clean is a challenge, though I have an education.

I was born in 1906, December 22nd, in the city of Yeketerinoslav, Ukraine.[2] At that time, it was 150,000 people; but now, maybe there's half a million. My father had coal mines in the Don Basin, and he was supplying building contractors in the city with coal and cement. He was quite well-to-do and a self-made man, very respected in the community, and belonged to the *gildis*—the "golden clan." You had to be quite well-to-do in order to be a *gildikupets*.[3]

The Jewish elite was exclusive, and well-mannered. They spoke French instead of Russian because the Russian was like a secondary language. They were not accepted by the Russians, but they had their own class. This is the *yichus*. For example, we once had a private teacher, a very proud teacher. Once Mama was walking with him, and this little son of a cobbler said, "Hello, *Rabbi*." And then a butcher came by and said, "Hello, *rabbi*." He says, "How come this urchin comes and says hello to me? I am a *rabbi*." So Ma says to him, "He honors you by saying hello to you. If you want respect, you should respect too."[4]

61

[There] was no Yiddish culture in our family. Mama couldn't speak Jewish well. Pa could because he came from a little village. But he always wanted to come to a big city. He struggled till he was eighteen. He found out that he had a rich cousin in Yeketerinoslav, and the rich cousin had sawmills. He wrote to him that he would like to come and acquire a Russian education, and the cousin said okay. But when Pa came, they wouldn't let him in the house, he looked so shabby; he had those earlocks and a long coat. So they put him in the bunk with the workers, but Pa said, "Well, you don't degrade me because I have pride." And he bought all kinds of books and started to learn Russian on his own. The money they gave him was not enough so he left his cousin and found a job delivering coal. He was quite adventurous; he was a go-getter. It happened that his boss asked, "You want to come and manage my mine?" It was in Petrovenki, on the Don Basin. So Pa went there. He hadn't worked there for more than five years when he became the head man and then he bought the mine.

My mother came from a very well-to-do family. Grandpa had saw-mills and a lumber yard. They lived across from Yeketerinoslav, across the Dneper, in a little village called Amur. It was on the shore off the sand dunes. When the river rose, they tied up logs into a raft and they put some furniture on it and lived on that raft until the water receded.

My mother was a beautiful woman and a brilliant student. She went to Russian *gymnaziia* and college in Yeketerinoslav. She studied languages; she spoke, oh, I don't know, maybe eight languages. In college, she was one of five Jews. Aggressive, strong character, that's for sure. Did we admire her? Very much. She was very liberal; and she didn't worry about religious convictions.

Mama wanted somebody who would look up to her, and Pa thought she was God herself. Whatever she said, whatever she did, was law. My sister the doctor, she's like Mama. Brilliant. My mother used to read night and day. She didn't know anything about housework.

Papa was very happy. He thought that he got the golden egg from heaven. She liked him, but she was always busy with us. And they didn't have much in common. Ma used to go to the opera and the symphony. Pa hardly went. She used to take us to musical recitals to appreciate good music, libraries to appreciate good books. She used to pack up the kids and go traveling to France, to Germany, Latvia, Lithuania, Turkey. We were all over Russia. Pa used to go to Odessa because he had arthritis—he used to go by himself. I used to say, "Why don't you go with Pa?" They were two separate people.

Mama was a good woman, and very generous. She belonged to all kinds of organizations to give charity.[5] She socialized with a lot of people—mostly Jews, but she had Gentile friends too. She used to lecture in universities on social sciences and history, so students and all kinds of people used to come. We always had people from the theaters, from the opera, from the symphony. Twelve o'clock at night the life started. Our table was always full.

Those were my mother's friends. Pa was not at her level and he was very money conscious. His friends were in *shul*. *Shabbes* was his time. Friday, after noon, he was never at the station [supervising coal deliveries]. He didn't go to those big *shuls*. Every holiday, they met in a small house and in the small house, just a *minyan* was *davening*.

We were eleven children—three girls and eight boys. Four died in the war and one just died in Russia now. He married a Russian girl and didn't want to leave. Only six came to America. I was the seventh child, the second girl. My sister was born after five boys in succession. She was admired and spoiled by everyone. She was the queen; I was always the goat. She was an honor student; I a mediocre one. She was taking piano and mandolin lessons while I was busy with the boys in the yard, playing ball. All my life since I remember myself, I was jealous of her. I think she's God. Yes. I never was jealous of anybody but my sister. I cannot understand why things come to her so easily and I have to work. And I was never pretty, and I was conscious of that. I always had an inferiority complex. But I was liked. But I couldn't reach Mama's height, and neither could I reach my sister's height, although I tried. But in the family, I'm the most capable. I wanted to accomplish the same as she did. Sewing and knitting and crocheting, which I liked very much —that I didn't want to do because I wanted to educate myself to be somebody in this world, so I would be independent. In case something happened, I wouldn't have to have a man to support me, I could support myself.

I was a wild child, and Pa's daughter. I valued my mother, but it was difficult for me to be like her. And Mama felt her children were tops. She wanted all her children to herself. She thought that marriage is a thing that you never miss: get your own life first. None of us married young.

We lived away from the Jewish community among the Gentiles on the outskirts of town. So all our friends were Gentile. We lived in an exclusive neighborhood. We had a big, elaborate brick house with big windows. It was beautiful. It was like a mansion, with servants, all Gentile, [wives of my father's employees]. We had an aluminum bathtub with a samovar for warming up the water. We had a toilet in our house, with a pull. We had gardens and fruit trees. There were stables for about forty horses. We had our own cows so we could have our own dairy. Pa had many workers, all Gentile; and he built homes for them near us. So we lived on extensive grounds.

And we children could afford to go to pretty expensive private schools—*gymnaziia* they call it. They were Jewish schools because the Russian schools allowed in only five percent of Jews. But the children of the better class of Russian Jews who lived in cities were all educated. [Our] principal was a Jewish woman, but we had Gentile teachers. [The school was] only for girls. And we had purple uniforms. We studied French, German, and Russian, geography, and history. We had gymnastics, and we had swimming and horseback riding. When we came in the morning, we had to say the prayer for the czar.

Now, no Jew, no matter how cultured he was, liked the government. I feel that every cobblestone in Russia is filled with Jewish blood. Absolutely every year, there was a *pogrom* before *Pesach*.[6] In big cities during the *pogroms*, they used any reason in order to get rid of you. As many Jews as they could kill, they did; but there were some Gentiles who would save you. We survived because Pa was a *gildikupets* and knew many wealthy Gentiles. But he was hurt many times.

The Cossacks were the most illiterate, wild, barbaric. They asked one of our best friends, "Do you know where a Jew lives?" "Over there." My mother was a heavy fat woman, and the Cossacks cut her dress open with a sabre. They took whatever they could and made fun of her. They came with bands and in the middle of the night, we had to hide ourselves—children under the bed. And they cracked Pa's skull because he was a Jew: "How much blood did you have to have for your *matzohs?*"[7]

Sometimes it was not the Cossacks, but the city *goyim*; they call it in Russian *istino russkii*, the true Russians. [Then] during the war, the Germans came and were raping women. The Bolsheviks were a relief because even if they confiscated everything from you, still and all, you were not afraid to walk on the streets and you were not afraid of being a Jew.

We suffered quite a lot. I don't know how we survived. Sometimes I don't even believe it's possible. During the Revolution, the Petlyura and Makhno bands were changing over.[8] Makhno was nothing but a bandit. And he was stealing from the rich. He called himself an anarchist, like he was supposed to give to the poor, but that wasn't so. They'd kill you because you're a bourgeois, a capitalist; and if you have, you have to give. We were not only frightened, we were frantic. It was a time of continuous fear.

So my brother built a shelter out of the cellar. We went by wagon to the forest across the steppe, five miles from our house. I helped him cut down trees for logs. We made bunk beds and brought whatever we could from the house—pillows, blankets, to cover the earth floor. Everything was provided for. We had candles; and as much in fear as we were, my sister would sit there and study. And Ma tried to teach us in order to get away from the fear, in case there will be schools that we will be able to go to. And that was our life.

During this time, one band was fighting the other band. Bombing. There was a woman who came from Switzerland to visit her children; it so happened that she knew about our shelter. By the time she came into the yard, they threw a bomb and they killed her. Right in our yard.

[After Makhno left,] I was hunting for food. I was real hungry. Oh my God! What I have seen with my own eyes. In the mud, dead horses were lying. With knives, people would take the meat and eat. Whatever they could find, they would eat—cats and dogs. Right in the dirt. People used to swell up and die, and they'd just decay because there's nobody to take them away. That's the most atrocious thing: to see people die from hunger. On one block, you'd see maybe five, ten people lying there swollen, asking for water (water was contaminated).

One night in winter, it was real cold, and bandits were in our yard. Mama said, "You have to run." She made us jump out of the window. Then she threw Helaine out of the window and we caught her. And she couldn't run—two years old, how could she run? So we took her by the hand and tried as much as we could in nightgowns! deep snow! barefoot! to run to the other end of town to a friend's house.

Another time, Petlyura came to town, a real gangster. That time, we were in the shelter. Pa walked out of it and saw that there was nobody on the streets. So we put on our clothes and we came to the house. All of a sudden, there was a big knock at the gate and bandits on horseback broke into our yard. And Pa said, "What do you want? I'll give you everything; just leave us alive." They grabbed my father and tied him up to a horse. My older sister came running and begged them to leave him and take her instead. So they whipped her so hard, she was all full of blood. Then they dragged my father on the cobblestones for a few blocks. We just don't know how it happened that Pa remained alive.

For a few weeks, it was quiet; school reopened. But the government was changing all the time. So one week, we would go to school, and then two weeks, we couldn't because there were fights in the streets. I was coming from school one day and all of a sudden, a grenade exploded and blew me against the wall. My whole side was full of metal splinters. My brother cut them out with a razor. I still have those scars.

When the Bolsheviks came, they were killing rich people. Because Pa was so good to his workers, they wouldn't let the Bolsheviks kill him. They protected Pa. So the Bolsheviks gave him a job managing the mines in Petrovenki. That didn't last long. So then he got into the hauling business.

The Bolsheviks confiscated half of our house and made an office there. I was working for the commissar of the Ukraine so we could get flour, butter, sometimes meat. I was eleven years old at that time. They taught me the secret codes, and, whenever a letter would come with secret codes, I used to decipher it. It lasted maybe six months. And because I was working for a big man, my sister was able to go to the university.

Then my mother made contact with my brother who lived in Omaha, Nebraska. We used to receive packages from him—Crisco and flour, dry cereals, sugar. They had to go through so many channels, by the time we got them, things had been taken out. We sold [some of it]. The neighbors came and asked, "How come you have so much to eat?" People were bartering with their remaining possessions. Give them a hat, a blouse, give them shoes, and they give you flour.

[Then] my brother wrote to us that "we'll try to bring you to the United States." There was nothing to live for in Russia; we didn't have anything. Money was not worth anything. Each band had their own money: one goes away; the other one comes. And therefore, it came a time when nobody wanted to take money. So Pa got diamonds in ex-change for our paintings and china and glassware. We hid the diamonds in the heels of shoes—even in my braids. Whatever we thought we needed for the trip was put on our wagon, and all of us piled on top of it. My brother drove us to the railroad station. It was a very emotional goodbye: tears in everybody's eyes.

We left Russia in 1923. I was seventeen. On the way to the United States, we had difficulties with our papers and we were delayed over a month in Moscow. Then we had to stop in Regitza, the border be-tween Russia and Latvia, [while they] verified our papers. They put us in the soldiers' barracks, and we stayed there two months. There were many more immigrants—we were not alone. Every day, we had to take a shower—you know, outside in the fields.[9] We had to be clean because there was a doctor and he had to examine us. No country would let you in unless your clothes went through fumigations, and they gave you inoculations and all that.[10]

There were delays and delays; we were afraid [my brothers would be drafted]. Then a man said, "Listen. Give me a sweater or whatever. If you have a pair of shoes or jewelry that I could sell, give me that, and I'll take you over the border." He wouldn't take money.

Five children with a grandma who was maybe seventy years old (I am sixty-eight now). Mama and Pa, too. And my American uncle's sister-in-law came and said to Pa, "Look. I have sixteen children; please take one. Maybe, maybe he'll be saved because I don't think we're going to be saved." So he took him—Stanley—too. And then our cousin who was living with Grandma. So we were ten.

At night, we dressed up, and we went through the mud and through the forests carrying leather bags and bundles. We had such beautiful leather luggage—it was so heavy to *shlep*, we left most of it on the road.

All night, through fields and forest; daytime, you couldn't do it because the border guards would see you. Other people went too; we were not alone. And some died on the road. Some had heart attacks; some got sick. It took two nights. Two days, we had to stay in canvas tents in the woods. This man supplied us with "food"—rotten apples. Feet were swollen and shoes wet. Until we got to Riga, Latvia.

And we stayed in quarantine there. They wouldn't let us in the city. But we had friends there. Grandma and Pa ate *kosher* with them every Friday.

Then we went to Germany. They locked us in the trains because of food riots. They wouldn't let us out. The train couldn't leave the station because demonstrators blocked the rails. There was a shootout between the police and the mob, so the train left.

Then, from there, we went to Rotterdam. We stayed there three days. We were also in quarantine. Then we came to Cherbourg, France, where we were to board our boat for the United States. [We found out] the quota was closed, so we couldn't go.[11] The White Star Line was responsible for us. They supported us all along because they sold us the tickets.

So they put us in quarantine in the Hôtel Atlantique. We were at least two thousand immigrants, maybe more: Czechs, Rumanians, Greeks, Turks, what not. There were dormitories and fenced-in yards with guards. You couldn't go out and you couldn't come in. Men's and women's quarters were separated by a gate. Every morning, at seven o'clock, a loud bell rang and we all had to go through the showers and have a doctor's examination because you couldn't go to the United States if you had a disease. Then we had our breakfast at eight-thirty. And there was a fellow, a waiter, who used to give us lectures. He wanted us to go to Israel. There was a section for the Jews that ate *kosher*, and we stayed there. Papa was very religious.

When we came to France, Mama worried very much. She wanted us all to go through school. That was the most important thing. She went to the mayor of the city and arranged for my sister to go to medical school in Paris and my younger sister to go to the *collège des jeunes filles*.

After about a year, we got out of the quarantine, and we rented an apartment on the ocean and lived there till 1929. We sold jewelry for money, and then Pa opened a liquor store in front of the Hôtel Atlantique, but he didn't make much. I was eighteen, and I started to work and go to school. My brother and I became interpreters. I was working at the Palais de Vêtement, a store for women, and he in a men's haberdashery.

In Cherbourg, there were no schools other than Catholic schools, and I went to St. Mary's convent. The nuns were the teachers. They taught me the piano, and French, and sewing, knitting, and crocheting. Oh, you have a religious education, naturally. In the morning, you pray, and after school, you pray, and when you go home, you pray; it's all the time praying, whether you believe it or not. One sister said, "You're going to remain here and become a nun." "But I'm Jewish." "You're not Jewish. You look like we are." "What do you think—Jews have horns?" "No; Jews are all thieves." She didn't even know what a Jew was. They were so ignorant, so indoctrinated with stupidity. Deep in my heart, I am prejudiced; I'm such a Jew you've never seen anything like it.

As soon as I grasped French, I went to the Sorbonne in Paris. My mother said that as long as we were detained, you may as well take whatever you want. So I went and took a course in general science, and I took up French in order to teach. We were three women and fifty men. I didn't mingle with anybody because I had to study. I came home and I ate and I was studying day and night. I didn't know when we were going to the United States, so I wanted to take in as much as I could. Nothing mattered to me anymore. I didn't care for clothes; I just kept on washing my own cotton dresses and trying to accomplish as much as I could in school.

And then papers came that we could go. My sister said, "I don't care, I'm not going. I'm going to finish school." And then later on, she became a doctor. But I had to interrupt my studies and go to the United States because that was our aim. A whole big family couldn't go at once—only parents to children and vice-versa—so Grandma and Pa went first.

Then, in 1929, when I was twenty-three years old and we were about to go, Grandma's girl, our cousin, caught encephalitis. So I took her to a private doctor. And he said, "They'll never let her go because she has Parkinson's Disease." We thought that Mama and the girl should go second class because second class doesn't go to Ellis Island. But they took them to Ellis Island anyway; on the boat, they found out that she is sick. My uncle had to put a ten thousand dollar bond [to show] she would not be dependent on the government.

Did you know about Ellis Island? It was a nightmare. We were met by interpreters, given entry cards, and taken to dormitories. After lunch, we were taken to a big hall for a lecture. They kept us three days because they had to look over the papers; they ask you all kinds of questions. It's an awful place; it's so morbid, it's like a dungeon. This one cries and this one faints and this one pulls their hair. It's such an awful place, you cannot describe it. During the day, we went in the yard and that was worse yet. Some children had to go back; they wouldn't let them into the United States. And some committed suicide.

[When you go through the gate to leave,] there are barricades and one goes at a time; you cannot look back to see who remains. They kept Stanley for a week because something was wrong with his adoption papers. Mama was in Ellis Island for a few months because of our cousin. Our cousin had no home until another uncle vouched for her and they got her out. They sterilized her; she was eighteen.

We took the Canadian-Pacific to Omaha. We had a big family there: my uncle was a cattleman and my brother was a butcher. Then we came to Chicago. Pa had a newspaper stand in Hyde Park.[12] He got two, three, four, five, six stands, and he made good money. We moved to a quite exclusive neighborhood.

Right away, I went to high school. I was working in a dime store besides. I learned English while I was going to school. I went one year and then I graduated high school.

Then I met a fellow who was working as a proofreader. He was good-looking. He came once with a straw hat and cane and a blue jacket and white slacks; he looked real chic. That appealed to me. He was so elaborate, so lavish, you know, after we hungered. I thought I'm walking on the clouds. I fell in love with him. And I got married. I was twenty-six. I don't think Mama liked it too much, but she didn't want to discourage me.

I was married for two years. I had a son in 1931, and my happiness was unlimited but didn't last too long. My husband was transferred to New York, and when he got to New York, there was no job because of the Depression. So my father said, "I'll give him a stand." But he wouldn't come; his pride was hurt. He wrote to me beautiful letters: "Without you, my life is not worth living."

[One day,] my husband's uncle comes and tells me he's married. I wanted a divorce. My womanly pride was stronger than my feelings toward him, and I didn't want him. I went to the criminal court and the man said, "In twenty-four hours, you can get a divorce." And that's what happened; but Pa says, "You have to get a Jewish divorce."[13]

It took maybe one year with all the investigations. I wanted to adopt my son (you know, a child belongs to the father). Pa had to take the *rabbi* to New York and talk to my husband, fill out all kinds of papers. And I had to go to four *rabbis*; [they're] sitting around a table, and I'm standing. Then they took me outside and I had to repeat after them what they were saying. Maybe it took five minutes, but to me it was five hours. And after it was all said and done, you have to bury your papers that you're clean again, that you can remarry.

I got remarried in 1942. We were working together at Goldblatt's [department store], and I met him and he was such a clean-cut fellow.[14] My father said, "A German Jew?" But I loved him and I thought to myself, "I'll take a chance." And I did. We're honeymooning for thirty-three years now.

And in my old age, I wanted to teach so I went to school and got my certificate. I was teaching adult education in the libraries. They told me I was too old to learn to drive a car, and I said I'm going to fool you [and I learned].

[I still remember] all the *pogroms* and all the atrocities that we went through, and my father saying he'd rather be a newspaper man and be happy than be rich and fear life. When we came to Chicago, he said, "This is God's blessed country and I want you every morning to thank God that you're here and I don't want you to forget it." It's still the best we ever had; of course, we have difficulties here also, but still and all, it's a wonderful land.

PART THREE

How They Fared

I see you, old woman. I see the *You*, not the old. In your eyes I read the story of the years, of the pain, the sweet delights . . . I know you, woman. Your blood flows in me. I am of your soul. The dreams you have dreamed come alive in me and in those around me. . . . But even as I look, your face turns into my own. We stand at opposite ends of the same long corridor, reflecting the image of one another.

I embrace you, old woman. And as I do, I honor my infants and those to come, my neighbors wherever they are, and the dawn which hides behind the nighttime of the present.

—Bert Kruger Smith, *Aging in America*

Anuta Sharrow

Anuta Sharrow: The Radical in Exile

Anuta Sharrow has been in exile for over fifty years. Her profound attachment to Russia distinguishes her sharply from the other women in this book. With more than a suggestion of longing, she describes Russia as the country of the socialist revolution and the center of the people's struggle for a better life, rather than the czarist empire which inflicted anti-Semitism. For years, she saw life in America as temporary. Her unhappiness here must have contributed to her romanticism about Russian culture and her intense identification with all things Russian. Neither time nor distance has severed her ties to her native country, where she has felt rooted all her life.

Although she characterizes herself as a "follower," she has not been passive. She may have been accommodating in her roles as wife and mother, but all her life she has "chased after" education and music. In contrast to the other women who speak easily of themselves and their personal experiences, Mrs. Sharrow is more at ease with abstractions. She has a definite sense of identification with history and movements.

Mrs. Sharrow is sanguine. While she speaks of certain people and events with regret, she is never angry. She is a disappointed romantic, yet she has a stubborn pride in her accomplishments and individuality. Looking back on her life, she can say with pride, "Whatever I could accomplish, I did."

WE DIDN'T WANT TO
COME HERE; we just were trapped, you know. We couldn't go
back. I had great hope that everything will stabilize and we'll go back.
And then the children were born, I got busy with the family, their
schooling, and this and that. So, a new experience in life. But it wasn't
a normal situation, you know; in general, it's not normal for anybody
that you leave your country and you go to another. It's a very disturbing
situation—they can't be happy; it's impossible.

I'm hardened already. I was very emotional; for years, I was emotional. It's a tragic chapter in a person's life, for fifty-five years not
to see relatives. All of a sudden you get a letter. My niece whom I left
as a baby in the cradle writes to me everything: how and when she left
my birthplace, when my father died, and what transpired there. And
her brother who was nine years old when I left him—he's a grandfather now. Mind you, when I see these pictures in my memory, ah,
what is going on inside. You can't forget, because often it goes through
you, through your mind and heart. Those moments, they are going to
live forever with me—what I had during my childhood.

You see, I was brought up in a small town, my birth town, about
eight hundred—Gornostaypol. Our town was something like a suburb
of Kiev, about ninety miles [away]. My father used to come for business and take me to a dentist [in Kiev]. Summertime, we used to take
the steamship: a *parakhod*, they call it. The Dneper, it's a terrific river
—wide and deep and long.[1] Overnight, something like six hours, with
the steamship. Wintertime took many hours because [we went] with
horses, with the sled. We didn't have a railroad. [On] the road to Kiev,
we used to go through villages and through farms, little towns like our
own.

In our town, the Jews lived in a separate section and the Gentiles—
you know, the peasantry—[lived] in a separate section in back of us.

So the Jews were about, I say, five hundred. We lived in a community; it's not like a city—you're together. The interests are together, and they unite you. It was a different life altogether, Quiet, nice, closer to nature, closer to the community. It was a happier life; oh my, no comparison!

The peasants lived in a backward way on their land. You know, there the peasants were exploited and they did the hardest work. Then came leaders, speakers, you know—idealists—and they told the peasants: "Fools you. Look at the rich people, how they live. The princes and czars, full of everything. Their dogs have a better life than you." That's the way they used to talk to them, like a father to a family. Lenin told them, "You must be educated," and they were educated because they found out that they have really a bitter, poor life. They didn't have even a doctor in their communities, and no schools. That's why I had to go to another city to enter a high school. So, and that was for the poor Jews too.

I remember when I was a child, there were lots of poor people. The Jews were poor because just a few were business people (the more capable, the more smart), but the rest they had to be a shoemaker, a blacksmith, or a tailor. Some of them were grocery people, some of them a little businessman, an artisan. They didn't make much.

I remember that my mother every Friday used to pack a big bag with food and send me to the poor. She knew where they were living. You know, in a little town, they knew the business of everybody. Oh, there you had to be careful. Every word and every move everybody knew, so it was a lots of fun. They used to gossip; they used to be jealous of each other, if one is richer and has more. I think it's a natural thing for a human being. It's a feeling of hurt why *they* didn't succeed.

Where we lived, it was like a miniature farm because we had a garden, an orchard, and we had our own cows. My family would be in the middle: I mean, not too rich, but not too poor because my father was a businessman, he made a nice living. That's why he could afford to send me to school, to Kiev. In comparison with others, they considered [him] a *nogid*.[2] (I didn't use that word maybe for sixty years.)

Our house—ah! if you would have seen the house. I wish I could show you. I can never forget in my life, it's vivid. The prettiest house we had. It was my father's dream to have a nice house. Ten years I know he gathered the lumber. I remember because they used to talk when the lumber is dry, it becomes just like stone. So we children used to jump around on the boards in the yard. Then finally, he got all the lumber and he hired a carpenter, and they put up the most beautiful house—believe it or not, the first one in that little town. It was the best because my father had a beautiful taste, an artistic taste. After they finished, I remember that he bought in Kiev a baby grand and beautiful furniture—stuffed.[3] I remember the color even, like a cherry red, brocaded. And two mirrors. It was a beautiful home—he loved beautiful things. One floor, but we had a concrete basement, and not everybody had it.

As soon as they finished the house, there was a fire, a big fire, summertime. The way they were carrying my baby grand—I was about fourteen years old, I was crying. And they put it out in the middle of the street, just to save it from the fire. And everything burned down, burned down. I have very bad memories about it. When I think about it, it's just heartbreaking. Then he built another house. The other house wasn't as beautiful.

I had a beautiful mother, and understanding; my father too was very understanding. He was an artist at heart, I'm telling you. He was a musician; and thanks to him that I know so much about music. He was very musical himself; in the army, he played trombone and cornet. In fact, they had a little orchestra of amateurs in Gornostaypol. He encouraged [me]; that shows you that there was a sense of culture, of art. He loved to go and listen to the *chazan*.

My father did lots of things. He was a manager for a widow's estate not far from us. And he raised cattle. He was energetic and used his brain. He liked independence. So he and a few other Jewish business people got together and bought a big house in the section where the other temples were, and they organized their own temple, a *people's* temple, not so much Orthodox because they didn't like the domination. My father wasn't a strict *Hasid*, no.

My mother and father were happy. My mother was very delicate, such a delicate face. She died when she was forty-six years old. I was about eighteen or twenty. There was an epidemic of dysentery. She told my husband when she was almost dying (that's what my husband says—he was present, we were students that time) that I should marry him.

My mother was a very understanding lady. She was just born with intelligence. Of course, it has to be developed, you know, by knowledge, by living. She wasn't modern educated. She knew Jewish and she used to read history, but she didn't know Russian [except to] speak it. [She wanted me to] perpetuate her own life, but of course with more education. Her ambitions weren't as great as mine, you know; she was happy because she had the four children (nice children we were growing [up to be]), and she had a beautiful home, and my father made a nice living. And you know, when a mother is happy, it comes back on the children to a certain extent. My mother gave us really freedom. We were not under discipline like here, because there it was not necessary.

I had two brothers and a sister. My sister was the oldest and helped in the house. Like half a mother. But such a devotion you can't find nowadays. She gave up her life for all of us and for my mother. After her was a brother Joe (Yosef in Russian). He was a businessman. He studied too, but he turned to business because he wasn't studious. My other brother, Sam, in the Jewish studies was a real scholar. He was a terrific Zionist but, let me tell you, he loved to read Sherlock Holmes.

I was closer to the Russian culture because that's all I did. I read Russian. I was advanced because I belonged already to the new generation. I loved my mother, that's true, but there was a gap between my mother and me culturally, intellectually. She belonged to the old-fashioned, to the Orthodox, because maybe she was afraid of God. When I was a child, I remember that in the morning she used to teach me to say a prayer. And I had to repeat word by word, you know, just like you take an oath or something. They used to read me history in those long winter evenings from the Bible and from Jewish history, in Yiddish. *Kosher*, sure and how! But I freed myself of that nonsense. As soon as I entered high school, that was an insult to the intelligence of a Jewish youth to keep *kosher*. I believe in traditions and culture; that's all right. But religion, no.

I was the baby; so everybody used to say because I was the baby, my father gives me so much. My father was anxious to give me education: musical education and general education. My parents themselves weren't educated [except in Jewish]. So they felt that would be a pride for their children to be, you see. That's one thing; the other thing, he was able to support me. He had the financial means to send me to school. I remember when I was a teenager, even younger, I said to my father, "I don't want any dresses, no clothes, nothing. Just send me to high school." They call it *gymnaziia* in Kiev.[4]

When I was about twelve years old, I started to study music and [to study] with private teachers. Then to high school, to Kiev. So most of my youth I really spent in Kiev; that's the capital of the Ukraine. I had a lots of private teachers. You could count on your fingers how many; maybe three or four. First, we had preparatory. When we were young teenagers, a teacher prepared me to the fifth class. And we Jews used to get together in our town. They were Zionist mostly. We had meetings and plays, like Chekhov and Andreyev.[5] The Jews were discussing socialism and their rights, and all that. We used to get together, recite poems and do other cultural things.

I wanted education, you see. Then, [so did,] for instance, my girl-friend Lisa. We were very close and inspiring in our town; we used to take lessons from the same private teachers. And she became a dentist. Then we drifted and I lost track of her. I didn't know how to find her and I was looking for her for fifty years [before I did find her.] She had memories with me. My life was quite connected, interwoven with her life and with the teachers and with the boys and with the girls in that community.

I was the only one in Gornostaypol, believe it or not, that took piano lessons. You know how I started? With a barber! How do you like that? When I was twelve years old. But the barber was very musical, you'd be surprised. He played everything by ear, and he had a nice position of his fingers.

I'll tell you, it's interesting, the influence of music. A neighbor of ours, a Polish woman, was anti-Semitic terrible, but she was a great pianist. At that time, I was ten years, eleven years; I wasn't mature musically. But she saw in me that I'm interested. Mind you, a little girl; she used to call me in and play Chopin, Bach. She graduated [from the] Moscow Conservatory. Me, she liked. And my mother every Friday used to send her a *gefilte fish* and a *challeh*. A great influence she had on me.

I was after music. From my childhood, I loved that. But of course, the Revolution, interruptions [of] all kinds. Then marriage, then children. But you know? After my children grew up, I went to Chicago Musical College four or five years. I was the oldest student, I think. I was a grandma already.

So my father was anxious to give me education. [One of] my teach-ers, he was a revolutionist. I liked him very much, and the best political education and general education I got from him. My way of thinking and the love towards the Russian culture is from that teacher. We used to sit till twelve o'clock and read all kinds of pamphlets. He was teaching everybody—it was a revolution. You know, he used to go out in the fields and teach the workers Marxism. He was in prison maybe three times for political activity. He was just one winter tutoring. He started me to prepare for a certain high school in Kiev because his sister graduated [from] that school. But he was too much active in the revolutionary movement; he didn't have time. He went to Paris to join other revolutionaries and prepare for the Revolution with Lenin and his wife, Madame Krupskaya.[6]

After he left, then I wasn't prepared enough because I had to have the examination for four classes, and it was very hard. For four! It's about six or eight years of study. So I had another tutor in summertime, you know. And that one prepared me. Then I came in the fall, in August, and I had exams and I could enter; they accepted me.

So my father got ambitious and sent me to *gymnaziia* in Kiev. There, lived a very musical family. Poperik was their name. My father rented a room in their hotel, and I had board and room in their house. I came during the winter. Those were the happiest days of my life. They had three children, all talented in music.

[My friend and teacher,] she's before my eyes. Her name was Bertha, and she was a first class talent—Jewish. I shared a piano; she gave me piano lessons. She really started me on the musical road.

So I lived in that house. I was a few years in Lissenko's school. He was a composer and a great nationalist, a Ukrainian.[7] Bertha Poperik was the first student in his school, and on scholarship. And she was my teacher. She played beautifully. We used to go together to concerts, and she used to give concerts. She had a great influence on me musically.

At that time, the Jews couldn't teach, they couldn't enter schools, unless they were very rich maybe. You had to pay for everything. That's why my father paid for me. I got the right [to live in Kiev] because I was a student. It was approved by the government. The school didn't belong to the government, but it was accredited. At the time when I entered, I was about sixteen years old already. They were wearing brown dresses and black aprons; and for examination, for a holiday, or a party at high school, we had white aprons—beautiful. I was in a girls' high school and the boys in a separate school. Jews there were quite a few—half and half, I would say, in my class. But the Jewish girl or boy had to know twice as much to give him a high mark. A Jew was hated.

I had friends, Gentile students, in Kiev, but they were not so close. Mostly I had a Jewish environment, you know, and [I was separated] in high school because of anti-Semitism.

We had a radical education [in Kiev]. [There were] reading circles preparing everybody for the Revolution. I didn't take an active part in the work. I mean, I just read and studied. There was a circle of other high school girls; together, we'd meet. They would have the same thought, the same philosophy, the same understanding. Most of them there were also Zionists, don't forget that. As I say, I followed because, you know, we girls get together and we had an influence on each other. I wasn't [a revolutionary]. I suppose the influence wasn't strong enough.

My husband was a student in Kiev, too. He studied privately, on his own, with a tutor. He rented a room at my aunt's house. That was 1907, I think. He was very good in mathematics. He was an *externi*.[8] They used to get up five o'clock and start to study. They were really the cream of the intelligentsia.

I went on vacation to Gornostaypol, to my parents, and then in August, I came back to high school. I was around seventeen when I met my husband there in the house (I also rented a room there). I was already in the sixth class. He was very intellectual. He ued to take me to lectures—only twenty-five cents, mind you. We liked each other. We were free; our life, our environment belonged already to the next generation and not the old-fashioned way. My father used to say, "First do your work and then go to the piano." I remember. I had a good background of housekeeping. In other words, he didn't want to make me feel that I am only for education and I shouldn't know practical things in life. He wanted me to be educated and all that, but he wanted me to marry a rich businessman or an intellectual or a professional. There, [it] was very hard to marry a professional, a Jew. I belonged already to the new, a different generation, and I didn't consider money is the most important. Just the opposite. If you like the person and you think you'll be happy with the person, you didn't think of money. There wasn't so much consideration as in the capitalist country.

But I'll tell you, here [in the United States] is more selection. There, in the little towns, Jewish women were limited. There were no schools;

so they were far away from the language, and from the Russian culture.
Only those that went to school in a big city like Kiev had a chance.
In the towns, they were locked up at home with the housework. And
there were lots of old maids, I'll tell you, because it wasn't easy to get
the right man. They didn't mix like now. "He's not good enough because
he's not from that and that family." For instance, an artisan—that was
a shame there. Idealistic [love] is only in poetry because they didn't
have problems. Nowadays, the women, especially in a capitalist country like America, are more free. They don't want to be slaves, and I
don't blame them.

In Kiev, I lived about five years. After I graduated high school, I
remained to study music still a couple years. After, I went to my home-
town and I myself became a tutor. Before the Revolution, I was busy
teaching: Russian, arithmetic, history, everything, all the subjects. In
the little towns like my town, I usd to come and organize a class of
girls, mixed [religions].

After the Revolution, they encouraged education. [If I'd stayed,]
I would have continued to teach music or Russian, because in all the
small towns, they were very, very short of teachers. Illiteracy was at
least seventy-five percent for sure, and maybe more.

So at that time I was tutoring, my husband had to serve in the army.
He was here [in America] five years: he ran from the army; he didn't
want to serve the czar because they were very anti-Semitic, and then the
war was coming on. We kind [of] separated. I loved too much—I was
very much attached to my family, to my people, and to the community.
He got a chance to come back. We corresponded all the time. For such
a long time—five years. And I was sincerely devoted and honest, you
know. I wouldn't do such a thing: to write letters "I love you, love you,
love, love, love," and go and get another boy.

He came back just as poor. Why he came back there? Well, because
I was there, and his parents; and he was also attached to his country,
to his people. So we married. You think we knew? This is a terrific
risk. We didn't know where we're going. At that time, all right, we were
young students, and we had intellectually a lots in common. That's
what we lived with. We were ashamed to talk about money; we didn't
need it—that was an era of idealism, and we were drawn in.

But I didn't even know how active my husband is. We used to go to
dramas; he took me to cultural meetings. You know, he was an amateur

artist, too. An actor. I fell for it—who wouldn't?—because I liked that, too. And he's a free thinker. I wasn't so young now, and time was flying, you'll be surprised. I was twenty-six.

My husband was happy to get me [with or without a dowry]. My father gave him a little money to start out, you know; and my brother gave some money. So he started to teach English there in Kiev. We lived in a furnished room. I studied. I'm—in Russian they say "a student forever." So I studied when I was young; then when I met him, I studied; then I studied when I came to America.

Of course, I didn't anticipate to come to America altogether because I loved my country. I loved the Russian culture, I loved my people and my family and friends, so many friends that we grew up and had schooling together and all that. Memories, terrific memories, you know. When you come young here with your family, you don't have that in your memory. But you come grown up, you are rooted in another country. My life was rooted in that country where I was born and I developed from my youth, from my childhood. I mean, we really didn't plan to come here. We were supposed to go just for about a month to Paris, a peace conference; we left everything in order to return back in a month, and we couldn't return back.

The minister of foreign affairs of the Ukrainian Democratic Republic, who was taking English lessons from my husband, recommended him because they needed a translator [at] a world peace conference. I had a chance to see Europe, so I was attracted, and when we are young, we like adventures, you know.

We traveled from Kiev. It was so cold. Oh, below zero because it was the first of January 1919. [At the conference,] there were French, Italians, Polish, English. That was a peace conference, but it fell apart. The civil war started. In Paris, we were only ten days. Right away when we came started a struggle there; somebody else took over the power. Those authorities that my husband was a translator for—the Ukrainian nationalists (the head was a more-or-less radical)—were not recognized altogether, so it fell apart, see.[9]

The generals Skoropadsky and Petlyura ordered *pogroms* at that time—they were something terrible. The governments were changing every five months until the Bolsheviki took over everything. The Revolution continued all the time, and we couldn't return back. That was the whole obstacle, you know, and the whole tragic thing. We didn't mean to stay here but we were locked out of our country. All depressed; we were stuck. We couldn't get letters, we couldn't communicate. I didn't mean to leave. I was crying I didn't want to come to America, but my husband, he talked it into me, and I trusted him. I was a follower; I was always a follower in life, you know. He's stronger. I was brought up like that.

My brother sent us money; and then we had some money too. They paid him anyhow, [even though] they didn't even have the conference.

From [Le] Havre we took the boat, but I was crying, I didn't want to come because I was afraid. America was something like somebody dies and disappears from the earth. But my husband says—you know, when you're young, you're tempestuous—for a month only. I had a brother here, and I was kind of attracted. To see America was very interesting. I remember even the boat: *Beau Rivage*, I think, was the name. Oh, beautiful for me it was—you know why? That's the first time in my life, I can never forget, I saw an ocean. Oh, my dear, that was terrific! You know, the waves and all that—the view. Of course, I was sick a little bit from the shaking, so all my meals I couldn't eat. And I was crying, "What I have to go so far from Europe, from my land?"

We came to New York first. There I had a cousin. But we stayed just a few days. Then we came to Chicago because we had an uncle— my husband's—and I had a brother. It was 1919.

So, but we adjust ourselves. My husband knew the language. We rented a furnished room; this was on the Northwest side. All the Jews lived there—most of them.

I'll tell you: when I first came, I thought it's a paradise. Even now; it's the richest country. Of course, all kinds of shortcomings in the government, but everything was in abundance. We didn't have any food [in Russia] at that time; we had to stand in line in Kiev to get bread. In America, plenty of everything. Technology and materialism. There in Russia was ninety percent the peasants; they didn't have the middle class altogether. Here is a middle class; the middle classes are not interested in Marxism. Capitalism's very strong here. Terrific strong. Here, they do everything for money. They'll give you poison in the restaurants; sure, they don't care. [But] you don't feel anti-Semitism here. When I was there, anti-Semitism was terrible. They were throwing little stones at me: "*Zhid, Zhid, Zhid.*" Believe me, I had a hard struggle. I felt the difference how the Gentiles are treated and how we Jews. I'm more a nationalist now than I was at that time. How do you like that? Because I suppose it has to do with the Jewish people that they felt inferior because they don't have education, and they are deprived of privileges. The government and all the Gentiles, they made them feel that way—they were anti-Semites. Oh, a Jew!

I was in the circles of the Russians when I came [here]. I held onto the Russian culture all the time. I carried the Russian culture with me, see. You'll be surprised—there were lots of Russians. Right away, I met two young ladies about my age. My husband knew certain people already in Chicago. You go to the neighborhood where [there are] lots of former Russians. Oh yeah, I met a lots of Russian Jews. The progressive people, we had literary organizations, a lots of them.

Of course, I had an aunt and a big family, and there I studied. They were like aristocrats. They knew the language, and they were Americanized already because they were so many years here. It was a nice home, an intellectual home. I used to come there, and they laugh, laugh, laugh, and I was laughing the way I speak. That is the only way to learn. You have to be aggressive in your language. Don't care if you don't say everything—correct yourself. That's the way to learn.

I never felt inferior because I'm a foreigner. No, never in my life. Why should I feel inferior? Let somebody come to Russia and start talking! You know, I don't think the foreigners felt inferior, but the Americans were so narrow-minded, they looked at them like that; they made them inferior.

And then my husband helped me a lots, and I got books. I went to schools, and with my books in Humboldt Park sit down on a bench or on the grass and study, study, study.[10] All the time. There was lots of lectures about what's going on [in Russia]. It's like going to school. I was writing from the books English, and then I went, when my children were growing, for a couple years to high school. [But] most of it, I learned myself.

My husband worked. He had various jobs and he was going to law school, but it wasn't easy. To me, [it] was a terrific loss to part with the music. So we got a piano in a few months; I started to study again. So I was busy with that, and I was busy studying the English language, and housekeeping.

But my husband was very restless. So he had a friend here. When he

met him, my husband was struggling from one job to another one; he
told him, "Prepare yourself for the Board of Transportation." In New
York. It's a short course of engineering. So he took that course and
went to New York and got a job. And I followed. That's why I call
myself a follower—he's a very convincing man. Now it's different. Now
he can't. I have my own strength—I learned.

We were always together; used to go all the time to lectures. He
used to lecture, he used to speak. Even now he has the talent. I don't
but I like other things better; you know how it is. There are certain
things he knows better, but there are certain things that I knew better.
For instance, I developed him in music; he never knew about music
much.

When we came back to Chicago, he graduated here from law school.
Then we went again [to New York] for four or five years. My husband
was on the radical side, and he was teaching in a school for workers.
He was busy with meetings; oh, he was active. When the children were
young, babies, I thought that he's more useful wherever he goes. I was
cooperating. Oh yes, I was submissive in a way. He wanted to be active;
all right, it's a good cause, you know. He was going and lecturing and
teaching—not for money. But [at] that time I felt [he] should be
devoted more to earn a living, to the family. But he was trying; I accepted that, I was the one that compromised. He was always busy, so
I was the babysitter. I was prepared for it; he's lucky that I was what
I was because I was responsible in life for the children, and I took care
and he didn't have to worry. But I didn't work; he had to provide.
There were times I would like to go to work but he didn't let me because he thought it would be hard on me.

Now my husband—intellectually, we have everything in common; we
like the same things. But to him, idealism in life was higher than the
material things, see? I am the opposite, maybe because I am a woman.
Not that I wanted riches—necessities. And we fell into Depression—it
was bad. Bad ten years. Just when the children were growing and needed
more. There was a time that we were on relief too.

After the Depression was over, he got offices; I didn't go to work.
I had too much work to do in the house. I studied and I also was a
tutor in music from time to time for grownups and children. I was
busy with my children, a house, and it's hard work. I loved my children.
I was happy. I mean I took good care, and that was everything in my

life. I lived for the children, I'll tell you. I'm just that kind of person
—maternal. My life would have been very empty without them. When
we started to move around and my husband had disappointments,
failures, you know that affects the children—their aims, their goals. I
think most of the time, most of the parents are a little bit disappointed
—very seldom when it works out the way they expect.

We lived all our life with hope that we would go there [Russia], but
our children were born and the children were getting their lives, with
school, with friends. So it was again hard for us to part with that
because they would suffer. And they didn't know the language, and
then it wasn't so good at that time to return back. Would have great
hardships with little children. You couldn't do that very well. I was
kind of rooted in *them*, my life. So that was going on and on and on.
You're in a safe place; it's very natural with a human being not to go into
a fire. That's the main reason why we remained here, and the reasons are
emotional. You know, whatever we lived through, it was very, very
bitter.

I like the United States. I love it. I almost grew up here. I lived here
more than there. But I'm still missing, I'm still missing my country.
Oh yes. And the friends. I'd like to see there and be there. Now I would
be afraid even to come there after fifty-five years. I'll come, what do I see?
Everybody's dead. I have a girl friend: she is old and blind; she has
glaucoma. In my memory, she's young; she was a beautiful girl, popular
and musical and loving. I'm telling you, the drama of life is something
terrible.

I am, you know, old—over eighty. I can't absorb and I can't do the
things that I used to do. But I still have the desire, you know—the
drive for [music]. [But] I wasn't two things. You have to have a com-
bination of two things: born talent, plus energy and a drive. I didn't
have enough of that. So whatever I struggled and worked at and could
accomplish, I did.

I'm very close to Pushkin. Ah, life works out, not the way you expect,
not the way you want, not the way you hope, and that's all. We have to
hope for the best and try and work for it. That's the main thing: don't
give up; don't be discouraged. I never was discouraged; see how natural
I am!

Mollie Linker: The Mother in the Community

Mollie Linker speaks about the meaning of motherhood—based on her experiences as a child relating to her own mother and based on her own experiences as the mother of two children. For Mrs. Linker, motherhood implies sacrifice for one's children, kindness and generosity to strangers, and responsibility and leadership in the community. A mother is the "backbone" of the family: she cares for the children, does the daily tasks of householding, and enforces tradition. Mrs. Linker's mother was the principal influence in her life, and it was her example she followed in raising her own children.

Mrs. Linker speaks with nostalgia of the old ghetto life and of its intimacies and hardships. For her, it was a place where Jewish traditions remained unquestioned and where neighbors formed a community in which each looked after the other. It was a melting pot in which people were unafraid of each other and the dictum to do and be good was taken seriously.

At seventy-four, Mrs. Linker continues to nourish her appetite for books. She is extremely well-read, and, at one time when she and her husband owned a school bookstore, she personally selected and read every one of the 750 titles they stocked. Her love of reading, coupled with her unwillingness to compromise her beliefs, her respect for tradition, and her loyalty to Judaism, have helped her to endure the hardships of her life.

Mollie Linker

I THINK THE WHOLE
STORY is about my mother. We were of a poor class. In Russia,
they would send their children to be like a servant [apprentice], even
the Jewish mothers. You were supposedly going to learn a trade, like
a dressmaker, but you had to take care of a flock of children and do
other things before you learned how to thread a needle. My mother
didn't want. She never sent us away from her. She wanted us to be
educated.

As you know, in Russia there was only twenty-five percent of Jewish
children that were allowed in public school. Boys were in a different
room and girls in a different room. Once you got in, you didn't pay—
it was a government school. My sister was two and a half years [older]
—we were six girls; I was the second. One morning, the teacher said
whoever will bring a sister, whoever will come first, that one gets in.
There was room for one more. And she ran—it was a cold day—and
when she came in the house, she couldn't speak, and she said to my
mother, "Dress her." My mother put a heavy kerchief on me, and we
both ran. And we came first, and that's how I entered school.

When I started school, I loved to read. As young as I was, as soon as
I could put the ABC together in Russian, I started reading. And I
would always pore over books. Do you know what I read at that age?
I read *Uncle Tom's Cabin* when I was ten; I read *Robinson Crusoe* in
Russian. I read anything I could get a hold of. And we only had one
room—it was with partition and with a curtain; and I would sit down.
We had a kerosene lamp, and in order my mother shouldn't see me
reading, I would get on my knees over the table and read, so I would
shade. She couldn't see me, but she would smell my hair—I had two
long red braids—singeing, you see. That's how much reading I loved.

And every time, I went for a book to the library twenty blocks away.
Near the library was a park, and in the summer, they had the army

91

band playing every night. I would take out a book, sit under the lamp, finish it, and then go home; and I got it good from my mother. It was a very beautiful old town called Rogacov in Moghilev state. What I remember of that town was that people came there because tuberculosis was very widely spread in Europe, and they came there for the pines—the pines were supposed to be like a cure.

We didn't have a house; we rented. You go to the open market on main street. The *mujiks* would bring in their wares, and you went and you bought things. You bought milk, potatoes, onions, and flour. It came after the High Holidays—October. If a man, a simple worker, had a sack of onions or potatoes, or a sack of flour and oil, he was rich. Meat [people] bought maybe a pound for a whole family; they each had a little piece; but we had plenty of salt herring and fresh fish —that was cheaper.

I remember instances of anti-Semitism. It was [during] the Russo-Japanese War. I must have been about six. I remember carrying lunch for my father—he was working. And in Russia, the winters are severe. You walked through trenches—the snow was piled up. They couldn't even see me; many times, I'd come home, my mother would pull the gloves off with my skin. You didn't feel it—it was a dry cold. As I was walking, a drunken soldier—a woman was walking in front of him, and he ripped her stomach up. I ran home screaming—I must have dropped the lunch.

I remember sitting by the window if my mother was away, and looking out. When it got dark, you close the shutters, you were afraid. You were actually always in fear because of big *pogroms*. In that town wasn't much, but there was the fear. I remember that scare that was in us all the time.

Then my father left for America to better himself. He was a scholar. He did work for a while as a bookkeeper in another town, but children were being born, you know. He had a sister here, and she thought maybe here he can do a little better; so she sent him a ticket. We came four years later, but my sister at fourteen, he took over a year before we came. And I was left with my mother and three other children, 'cause the sixth daughter was born here.

We struggled very much. My mother's parents were far away; they couldn't help her and she was too proud to tell them. She never wrote and said she needed help. I must have been ten. I overheard the woman where we lived—the landlady—say to her husband, "The man went to America; she's with four children here, and she's sick. What if she dies? What are we going to do?"

And I remember, my mother knew a woman—a Polish woman— and I ran to her and I told her. She came and said to my mother—she was a widow with three girls and a boy—she says, "Look. We're both alone and I need you." And she gave her a little house, one room; it was in an orchard, and she said, "I'll charge you two dollars a year rent." And she'd bring in milk from the cow, and we played together, the kids. Apples and plums would fall in the window. She was so good to my mother. She had that house ready for her. She was a Gentile woman, and she was wonderful, kind.

And that's when my mother started sewing. My mother never knew how to do a thing because she was raised with maids in a village where they had a lot of cheap help, and she was the baby. So she learned the hard way. That's why I say she was something, my mother.

When I came here, I was thirteen and a half. The train we were going on stopped at Vienna for about a week—that was an immigrant hotel. There was in our hotel a nice-looking boy and he said to me, "Do you want to go to the wintergarten of Franz Josef?" and I said, "Sure. I'm going." I was always looking for new things; I was a very pretty, big, husky girl at thirteen. As I was walking down, I felt myself get yanked by my braids and my mother said, "You're staying here."

In Brussels, Belgium, we stopped off, and my mother almost lost me 'cause I had to see everything. And I saw beautiful two-story houses —I'm here sixty years and I can still go back and remember— and from Brussels, we went to Antwerp. That's where we got on the boat.

We came here in April 1914. Our boat—either it was torpedoed or [something happened to] the stern—but instead of going through Ellis Island, the natural way, we were sent out a tugboat, pulled us into Halifax, Canada. Those things I remember just like they were now. And that was the largest boat that came across. I guess the war was already going on in Europe; we had thirty-seven nationalities on the boat.

And I was always a fighter. My grandchildren call me the Communist, the rebel. Naturally, we were third class [on the boat], you know. What did they give us to eat? Well, most of them were strictly Orthodox so they couldn't eat meat anyway, so they gave us herring and potatoes.

But I always wanted to see a lot. I came up on the deck—I always used to be on the deck to see fish and the ocean. That's how I met the captain; and I must have sneaked down one day in the first class or second, I saw children were given fruit or candy; and I came up and spoke to the captain. I was not afraid. Probably I spoke in Russian because we spoke Russian more than Jewish. And I said to him, "How come there are so many children down here and they don't get fruit or candy?" The next day, there was a big basket of fruit and candy for the children. That was my first fight.

So, as we stopped off in Halifax instead of Ellis Island, we had to cross the border. Our train crossed from Canada into Detroit; we crossed on the ferry. That I remember, too. When we came here, my sister, with the help of my aunt, already had an apartment for us in Chicago in the Old West Side with dishes and everything. The Old West Side was started on Canal Street, Maxwell Street. It was large families. The fathers worked, the mothers worked at home, cleaning, scrubbing, cooking, taking in boarders, if they couldn't make it, and did their shopping. Then there were quite a few Jewish merchants on Olson Street. There was a beautiful *shul* where we were, near Roosevelt Road and Ashland—it was the most magnificent building, with lions. It seemed to me that there were beautiful brownstone homes. They called it *Deutschland*.[1] We lived above stores. It was like a third floor, and we had to walk up. It was a big apartment. One bathroom to six rooms. You had to heat your own water. We lived in a mixed neighborhood —a lot of Italians, and some Polish people. But we got along nice when we lived there.

We struggled. We lived poor but very clean. Right after Passover, I entered school. When school was out in June, I knew I couldn't go back anymore, so coming home I cried all the way; and I was put up in high fifth in less than two months—it was just the language I needed most.[2] They had immigrant classes to teach you the language. And I came home, it was on a Friday, and I said to my mother, "Ma, the teacher cried," and I broke out sobbing, because I liked school. My father had a job for me. I couldn't do anything—at that age, you know, you couldn't work till you were sixteen, but kids worked at four- teen and at thirteen.

So I was a tall big girl, and there was a job for me in a glass factory. I was cutting glass; I'd come home, my hands were cut up. We were cutting out little round [pieces] for frames, not for eyeglasses. And it would slip and you were handling glass. The conditions of working girls were very bad. When I worked, I worked twelve hours a day. The pay was twelve dollars a week. In my shop, we had little gaslight fixtures—you couldn't see what you were doing. My shop was in the back of a big store. Everyone was a little boss for himself, and they exploited the people. There were a few women and men working there. They told me when the inspector will come, I'm to tell him I'm sixteen. Well, I looked sixteen. Who should know the inspector is a woman? So I tell her I'm fourteen. It must have cost them plenty to get out of it.

And I started night school. I went for about nine months. I got up at six in the morning; I went to work at seven thirty; I came home at seven; and school started at seven thirty, and there was a few blocks. So I had just time enough to wash up and change a blouse . . . I had two blouses. And with a sandwich, I went to school.

I fell in the basement of the glass factory. I injured my leg. And about six weeks later, I felt I couldn't walk. I wouldn't tell my mother. So I had to stop from school; I was in the hospital for maybe two months. If I waited two more days, I would have had the leg taken off. The bone was infected. We didn't have money for a doctor, so my mother took me to the clinic. As I'm sitting there, there's about twelve young students and a head doctor. As they're examining me, I'm getting red in my face, I was so embarrassed and I point, I says, "It's my foot!" Then someone must have told my mother to tell the boss 'cause it was his factory and he probably had insurance; I had a private room, everything was taken care of.

From then on, my sister took me into Hart, Schaffner, and Marx— that's men's clothing. I was given something to do on the machine. On big overcoats, I had to do a certain stitch. Piecework. Each one does something else on the overcoat. I was very fast. The machines were all in a row. And it was so hot, not even a decent fan. And you had these big heavy winter coats on your lap, and you worked, and you sweated. Windows were open, of course; flies too. You had a little half hour for lunch (we worked close to ten hours). And you talked. But you kept so busy and the machines were roaring—the machines were in back of you and the pressers were in back of you—but you talked. You had to be careful not to stitch your fingers in.

That's when they started to organize the Amalgamated. Each floor had a shop chairman. The president of the union worked in our factory. As you worked, you joined. We went to meetings and dances. There was a union hall. With the union, we worked shorter hours. They tried to make a social life for the young people, and they would have picnics in the summer and while they had the picnics, they would lecture. Once I remember going to a dance. Well, I was romantic, just like all young girls. Where I worked, there were two brothers who were the shop chairmen, they used to come and inspect your work. They were as handsome as any. They probably were twenty-seven; to me, they were old, you know. And I was asked to dance from one of these fellows. Well! So you see, girls always have dreams.

At fifteen, I took almost three hundred people on strike. Must have been [there] about six months. The building was an old tall building and there were only two small elevators. So whoever got in, got in, and the rest couldn't get in. [Then] one wasn't working and they didn't bother to fix it. You had to wait a long [time] or walk to the fifth floor, or they'd be late to work. You wanted to make your money; you were working piecework. Some people couldn't walk up that high.

And one day, it dawned on me—why should these older people, old men and women, walk up to the fifth floor? I stood up a couple of times; I says, "Let's go to the union." The foreman wasn't around—you'd get fired. I think they must have been flabbergasted that a young girl can do things like that 'cause there was no comment—we just went. We marched all the way to the union. That day we stayed out of work; there was no picketing. The next day, the elevator was fixed; and then we used the elevators. That's why my grandchildren call me Red. I was always doing those things.

There was mostly Italian women and girls [working there]. As you know, they're lovers of music. About once every week, we used to go to the old Auditorium; we were up in seventh heaven. And the garlic smell was awful but they liked it. I saw operas. We went straight from work. Everybody watched over me; they all liked me. I was one of the youngest ones.

When I worked there, already I was sixteen. After working about a year and a half or more, I was bringing home about thirty-five, thirty-six dollars a week. That was a big pay. I gave it all to my mother. It was the respect to bring and give your mother the money. It was the mother always there.

And the love for reading was always there. So I read the [New York *Jewish Daily*] *Forward*; I would pore over books—biography, Mary Antin, until my sister or my cousin would pull me out to go someplace.[3] We'd go downtown. Saturday afternoon, when we had to go to Field's on State Street, we girls would dress up. Summer, we'd take the street-car and the Elevated and go to Jackson Park. And there were dances, there were parties, boys and girls. There was more singing than anything else. There were pianos in most of the homes. We would sing American songs in English. You see, we all tried, even the parents, to speak English as much as we could. We sang songs, we played games. There were kissing games, too. Post office! I didn't know what it was all about, so naturally, all the boys, they would take me Post Office.

[In our family] we were all pretty girls. We really were, every one of us. When I must have been about sixteen, my father used to have our pictures to show off at work. Well, my parents thought I was the prettiest of the lot; they didn't show a preference but. . . . So this young man, when he saw my picture, he said to my father he wants to come and see me. He must have been twenty-seven. And you know how many years ago this was—maybe sixty 'cause I'm seventy-four—I'm not ashamed to admit it. So he came to the house with a car. Everybody, through the curtains you know, was looking out because a car at that time was something. You ran after it like you saw the first train. The house was immaculate—very poor, but immaculate. It was a happy home. And he looked at me and I guess he said something the next time to my father. So my father said to me, "Mollie, do you think you would care for him?" And I said, "Pa, no." So this is what he said to me, to bring out that they did not force us to marry who they wanted—there was no pressure. "You know, he's got a factory. It'll be good for you. You'll have everything your heart desires. It'll be good for me, too." And I said no. I had a lot of suitors.

So this is how we struggled, and this is what I saw. The younger sisters, they had it easier already. They finished grammar school; they had two years of high school. It's the older ones in every family that had to help out. My mother was something great in our family. Everyone looked up to her. She had a piano in the house and a violin for the younger ones. She went without shoes, without personal things, but the fifty cents a week for the piano was there. [Being a woman was] hard work. You didn't have the washing machine. You didn't have electrical appliances. If you baked, you had to beat it by hand. When you washed clothes, you had a big washtub; and if there was no basement, you put it on two chairs with a washboard and you washed clothes and you hung it on the porch. If not, you washed clothes in the bathtub. She was the one to shop, to cook, to sew. And to see that the girls are dressed right and to watch over the girls. Most of the men, I believe, at that time left the bringing up of the children to the mothers.

Our house was always filled with friends; and my mother loved it. You didn't make no *hors d'oeuvres*, you didn't make no fancy Jello molds; whatever you had, you offered. *Chanukah* parties were in our house. My father would change two dollars in nickels and dimes, and throw it, whoever grabbed it. And there were always friends. The family was small. We did not have anybody here except mother's cousin. And on my father's side was the aunt and her family. That's all. And we just had our own family. We would talk. There was no radio, there were no TV's; we had a gramophone. We had holidays. On Friday nights, when my mother lit candles, my father said a prayer over the twist of *challeh*. There was respect. We never started eating before my father made a prayer. And holidays were observed and they went to synagogue—couldn't afford tickets for everybody.[4] And the meat was supposed to be *kosher*.

My mother wanted to be in the better neighborhoods because of the girls, always going a little higher. [We moved] three times. That was the immigrant woman. She wanted always something better for her children, especially for girls. The father went out to make the living; the mother was the backbone of everything. They think about women's liberation—I think that the mother, the immigrant mother, was a real woman because the children looked up to her, the community looked up to her 'cause she was the leader. She was raising her children. She was encouraging them to go to school. She was encouraging them for music, and the better things in life.

The Jewish mother to me was like my mother. She went without personal things; she didn't smother us—she was very strict with us. She gave us a clean home; she gave us encouragement. She went to school, and we respected her. She made our dresses—we were the best dressed girls. And she cleaned and she washed and she cooked; but she didn't cling. We never heard, "Shut up." We never heard anything like that in our home, and that's how I raised my children. She was aggressive to the extent where she wanted to better herself. She was the leader of the neighbors. If somebody needed something, she was there. There were no charities like now—it's the women that got together, collected food. When they saw a woman in the butcher shop or the grocery not buying enough and they knew how many children she had, my mother would go to a few neighbors, collect money and bring food, and put it under the door and walk away. Somebody came in, they wanted to eat, or a beggar, you sat him down at the table, you made coffee. If you had bread and butter or a piece of herring, whatever you had, you offered it to him. My mother did it. My mother did an awful lot. We had the best teacher, and that was my mother.

In 1918, the flu broke out, but bad. In every house, there was a patient. They didn't know what to do. My mother had an apron in every house, and this is what she did. This I want people to know— what mothers of that era did, and the respect they got. I was married, I had a little store. My husband was working—you can imagine how much the store was taking in. She would call me through the window and say, "Molly, come take the temperature of so and so." I put a lock on the store, go upstairs; she'd wash my hands, put something over shoes, and take the temperature, take the bedpan. There were two telephones on the whole block. I had one, and somebody else; [she'd have me] call the doctors. That's what my mother done. See women— they were not afraid.

But it was always that we took care of our parents. It was a different life. There was more respect. The love was there. We didn't sit down to eat until my father sat at the table.

And my father, of course—he left it all up to my mother. He loved her very much. As for her marriage—she never knew him before. She just saw him maybe a week or two before they were married. It was arranged marriage because he was a scholar from a very fine family. My father was a great debater. He used to sit down and talk to us of the *Talmud*. When he got married, he wasn't quite twenty-one, and he was in the theological college. And he didn't get the last degree to be a rabbi. He spoke fluently German, Yiddish, Hebrew, and Russian. And he came here, he spoke English. He fixed umbrellas.

I got married at eighteen in 1918. I knew Henry, my husband, for more than three years. My honeymoon was spent in the back of a candy-store. We worked side by side for fifty-five years. We lived across the street [from each other]. Someday I'm going to write a story about that street. It was one big street: we had the melting pot there. We had German, we had Swedish, we had Italian, Norwegian, and Jewish. [We got along] beautiful. In summer, you'd sit outside and talk. We scrubbed the sidewalks; it was so clean. They called Jews something, they beat them up—but it wasn't so important. It wasn't an undercurrent; they called you what you are and that's it.

This is how I met my future husband. There was a shoemaker next door to us. So I went down to have my shoes fixed and my husband came in, and I said to the man, "How long will it take to fix the heels?" He says, "Oh, a couple hours." I says, "How will I go home?" So Henry pipes up, "You can take my shoes." That's how our courting started. We played ball across the street; and it went on for three years. They called us Romeo and Juliet. We used to call to each other from our windows. We went to a dance; we used to go quite often. It was either an organization (the *landsmanshasten*) or a union dance. We went in the armory, a big place on Taylor Street.

I really can't express up to this day what love is, you know what I mean? They say like Romeo and Juliet and Elizabeth Browning. I don't know. Whether you get used to a person, whether it's physically, I really don't know. Now I know that I looked up to my husband. We had a very nice life. And he respected me and I respected him. I guess love comes, with caring and doing things for each other.

[For my trousseau,] here is what happened. Mothers of that era have the peddlers. The peddler would come in the house. She would take six sheets, tablecloth; pay out fifty cents a week. You bought everything on payment. So when I got married, I got six sheets, some pillowcases, tablecloths. And the wedding was in back of the store—we already had the store, a little school store and candy store. It belonged to my husband's side of the family.

In that era, the women that didn't go to work had a little business. That's how you helped your husband. If you had to help out in the store, you were still home. My father-in-law said to me—years ago, was a shame to go to work—he says it was all right to stay in back of the store and help in business, that was nicer than going to work. I didn't feel it was right for me to work when the two children needed me. So [if we didn't have a business] I worked in the neighborhood in a bakery.

Our life was so different. We were never just business people. We were neighbors to all. If a child didn't have any money—if I saw one buy and the next one didn't, he got the candy anyway.

But we moved a lot because we had one store here, one store there. My husband was a laundryman in between times. I lived once with my mother with one child, and then I came back with two because of circumstances. We were moving north to mixed neighborhoods. We had trouble. In certain areas, we couldn't get an apartment. In Albany Park no Jew was allowed. Right on the outside [of the building it said that]. It was a pretty hard life. And I did my own cooking, my own sewing, my children were dressed beautiful. I always read. I went back to school in the afternoon. My hand was always up because I knew the answers.

Then we had a store in Evanston. A woman came in with ten girls, and those girls were taken away from broken homes. So when I found out—we had games, we had books, we had magazines, we had things to make—I gave it to them for cost. This is the kind of people we both were. Of course, when my husband got sick, everything went. But I don't regret it because we have friends all over town. He had a hard life and I had a hard life. We worked together and we loved being together.

I keep a strictly Orthodox home, the dishes and everything. I feel like I'm obeying my tradition, from my father's and mother's side. And I think I like it, too. I think I respect it and I love it. It's the heritage; it's embedded in me. I'm not going to change. I feel that I want my grandchildren to remember me, say, "My *bubbe* or Grandma did that," just like my children remember what my mother did. So it isn't hard for me to have my Passover dishes and make my traditional *Seder*. It's not hard for me to have dinner at the High Holidays. As long as they respect me when I come. Their home is theirs. My two daughters, it's their home, I don't tell them [what to do]. But they give me respect and I give them respect.

But maybe keeping *kosher* isn't a good Jew. It doesn't have to be. [But you have] to be good and *tzedaka. Tzedaka* means to help a person, to help you do something. In our heritage, the first thing is *tzedaka*. It started even in Europe. If one came to your house, you helped him if he stretched out his hand.

I was invited to speak about Russia [by] my granddaughter Linda's professor. When I walked in the hallway of that building—I call it a "house of learning"—I felt myself ten feet tall that *I* can walk in such a "house of learning." I didn't have the opportunity. And that I told them—how I felt walking in in that building. And my regret, I always regret—I should have gone back to school, and I should have kept up. But then I got married young and I shackled myself to the store. Then the babies came. We worked eighteen hours out of twenty-four. I lived in back of the store on and off. But I was always happy. I always thought there was somebody that was worse off than I am, see? At my age, at that time, what could I do? So I worked in a factory [at first]. But if I would have had an education, with my mind, if I had the time, I probably would turn out to be something else. But then later on, you're content with your lot, and maybe sometime there was a rebel in me. Yes, yes. The independence came from education: that you weren't afraid; you could go ahead and try and do anything.

Beatrice Pollock: The American Par Excellence

The relative ease of Beatrice Pollock's entrance into the American middle class separates her from many other immigrants. She is justly proud of her English, and her concern with its proper use is a clue to her standards of relative status and education. She is a convincing representative of those immigrant women who, while retaining many of the values of their parents and native cultures, also accurately reflect the values of contemporary middle-class America. Her wealthy sister and her own marriage to a professional architect no doubt contributed to her ready acceptance of American standards for the good life.

While the facts of her life are not so different from those of other immigrant women, some of the circumstances are, as is the context in which she places them. For example, when she recalls her youth, she chooses to remember her past achievements rather than the miseries of her life in Poland.

Despite her identification with the middle class, she rejects a materialistic approach to life and is sensitive to those values she feels create a loving and kind person. All through her life she has seen herself as a purveyor of love and understanding, as an individual who defines her purpose in life through her social relationships. Perhaps because of this attitude, at seventy-two she has not lost her youthful optimism and does not feel shunted off into a segregated world of the useless old.

WHEN I CAME, it was just like coming to the new world. My God, there was no comparison, particularly for Jewish people.

My father was here when I was born. He was here for four years, and it was hard for him to get started. And he left his wife and children, and he felt that what's the good bringing them. You know, you come, and you don't know the language—he was a brilliant man, educated, but it didn't do him any good. He tried everything; it didn't work and he was very lonely for all of us. He managed to have enough money to come back.[1] He didn't like the States; but for me, he thought it's wonderful to come. He used to talk to me as a little girl, he would love it if I came here to this country. I didn't comprehend why he was saying it, you know.

[Russia] was terrible. Except I didn't quite understand it when I was there. Everybody was prejudiced. And my family—my uncle, my cousins—what they went through to become a doctor. A Jewish person to become a doctor is like pulling teeth.[2] They had to go under false identification because they went so far they dreaded the thought of losing it. My father was a businessman and he traveled a lot; he'd purchase all kinds of things like for the grocery people. There was some kind of a [problem] somebody got into with him. He lost [a court case]; he had to pay $400 and I remember how my father felt. He says, "If it would have been my fault, I'd accept it, but these people . . ."

Nobody, nobody wanted to listen to you. There was one family, and they were supposed to be the elite, you know; they *thought* they were. And they liked me so they wanted me to be friends with their little girl. So my father said: "Well, I don't particularly like them, and I don't think they like us, but give it a try; if they're nice to you, why not?" So I tried. The little girl was very nice but the mother was always so

105

critical; and so once she said to me, "Do you know how to read Russian or only Jewish?" I said, "Give me a book, I'll show you." Of course, I learned how to read Russian and I learned how to read Yiddish and Hebrew. So she became a different person and tried to act very nice. One time, the little girl came over and she was hugging and kissing me. She says, "You're my best friend. I'm going to tell you a secret. *My mother hates you.* You know why she hates you? Because you're Jewish." So that's what you lived through in Russia.

I was born in a very little primitive city, Motol [near Warsaw], but Motola in Jewish. And there was one part of it for Jews, and the other side for the non-Jewish people. There were about 200 Jewish families —we were really a small percentage. We didn't mingle with the [Gentiles]; they didn't mingle with us.

Nobody was really considered poor, because they had their own little houses, built by themselves. I don't ever remember worrying about food or clothes. And when you live in a little town like that, if you have your own home, and you have food, you don't really ask for more. We had a large house—we had a little extra [room] that we were able to rent to someone: a couple and two children. We had a store. I used to help my father. And I'd sneak in a few things, a cup of sugar, and give them [to customers] without money and they used to love me for it, of course!

I had a tutor, and then my friends started to go to school, so I started to go to school, too. Everybody [in a] huge room. Didn't get much of an education unless you tried yourself, very hard. I used to read a lot and I tried, but I wasn't pleased; I told my father many times that one man cannot teach a great big class like that—it's ridiculous. Actually, I did beautifully regardless of the system.

My mother died when I was about five—her heart. She was pregnant, and the doctor said definitely she cannot have a child. And you know in Russia, Jewish people are very Orthodox. Stick to your religion, whatever. And she wouldn't have an abortion, no matter what.[3] My father was pleading, begging, had the right kind of a doctor in a different town, had it all arranged, and she wouldn't go through with it. So when the time came she was ready to have the child, she died. Just like that. On the floor. The little baby was out of her already, but dead. That I'll never forget either. She was lying—and I gazed up to her, thinking, she's resting on the floor, it's kind of strange; but I bent over, and there was the little baby in her arms, and my father picked me up, told me to get out of the room. But I didn't quite comprehend that she was never coming back.

And when I was five years old, I walked to the cemetery, where there was a big picture of my mother; I wàs there for about an hour, talking, crying—somebody picked me up and took me home. Then I realized that my mother is never coming back.

After my mother died, it was getting very difficult for me. As a child I suppose I was jealous because I'd come and the mothers would wash the little girls' hair—and they'd look so beautiful. And I didn't have anyone to do all this luxury for me when my mother was gone. So I think I had a very difficult childhood.

My father got married 'cause he was miserable, but he married the wrong woman. And I had a stepmother.[4] She had nothing in her heart. [She had children, but] she left them— in a different town with relatives. That woman—ooh, I don't know why my father married her. He was a wonderful father; he loved all of us and I think that used to kill her—she couldn't stand it. The minute she'd see him come near me there was such a vicious face on her that as a child I knew that there was something. When she came I was almost six. She used to grab the books out of my hand and try to make it as horrible as possible.

I never told my father all the things she tried to do to me. She walked by once with a pot of mashed potatoes for herself and I was sitting and reading in my own little bedroom, and I smiled just out of kindness. I didn't want to argue with her even at my age. She grabbed the spoon she was mashing the potatoes [with] and threw it in my face— hot, boiling. So I didn't say anything. I cried; she walked away, she didn't care. Then my father came home, and every time he used to walk in at night, no matter what time, he'd lift me up and kiss me good night, and he felt it. He says, why is my cheek so hot? So I never told him. I hated to hurt him.

Then the children came to visit us. That I'll never forget. Two girls. And I had hostility in my heart—because of their mother. But when I met them—they were so sweet that I started hating their mother more than ever. You know, when people can't care about their own, how can she care about anyone else's?

During the war [World War I] the Germans got in first. I was only twelve years old, but I was as tall as I am now. I'm 4'11", that's how I was all my life. So they used to have dances, and they were so wonderful; you know, like some people say, "Oh, the Germans . . ." but it's not so—the fact that Hitler and all that doesn't mean that all Germans are bad. The German soldiers were so sweet and docile, I remember. They used to treat me like a little queen.

I had a boyfriend. His parents were very wealthy. And he was five years older than I and he was away in different schools. And he really got a wonderful education. And I thought he was terrific until I came to this country and I met my husband. I really must not have [liked him]—just he was the elite in town and my father wanted it, you know. He hoped there will be a marriage.

We met across the street; that's where he lived. We started dating; he used to come every night except Friday. There was no place to go, no show. There was a party, maybe once in two years. You'd come and sit around and the parents were watching you. My father always trusted me—you know why? Because all he had to do was look at me, it meant I had to come in and my boyfriend knew it too. But still, everybody did everything they wanted to do, only the parents didn't know it. Sometimes at night before really dark we'd take a little walk —I'd see boys and girls hiding in under the trees and doing all that.

I don't say I had any sexual intercourse with my boyfriend, but he kissed me and hugged me and my father didn't know it. Once we were sitting . . . we had a little house with a beautiful porch; it was dark. My father walked up and saw him kissing me on the cheek. We didn't kiss on the mouth—there was no such thing, just innocent little kisses. So my father didn't say a word. He got in the house, and the boy said, "Uh-oh, you better go in." I got in the house and my father was sitting in the kitchen—he made something to eat; I thought he's never going to say anything. And meanwhile the boy was so concerned—it was something I didn't expect from anybody really. So he sent a letter to make sure that my father will read it, that my father will know he's not fooling around with me. So when the letter came, my father opened it. He was reading and smiling and smiling and reading. He says, "Yes, I don't mind, don't worry about it, but don't stay out too late."

Then when I got older, and I was already seventeen, my father started to talk about me going to this country and I looked at him and I said, "Why do you want to get rid of me? Why? I'm happy." You know, after all, when you're young and you know your neighbors, they're like family; and we lived near the river, a beautiful river, and the minute summer started in May, the girls had one place to swim and the boys had another place. We didn't wear bathing suits so the boys had to come and look at us, of course, and we used to run home and tell our fathers and mothers, and they used to go back to the boys' parents and try to settle it, but it was a good life.

When I left, [my stepmother] disliked the idea of my father's coming to Warsaw with me, to make sure he saw me off. I didn't say goodbye to her—just moved out of the house. I was eighteen years old already. I was there [in Warsaw] for three weeks before I was able to go. I was scared to death. Suddenly you saw cars and I never saw one before. I got on my boat, and it was kind of frightening for a young girl who's never seen anything but the little town on the ground. I came in 1921.

My sister brought us here 'cause her husband had a lot of money. I was like her child; it wasn't like a sister. There was eleven years difference in our ages; and when my mother died, she took over and she became my mother. And my sister did not want to marry the man she married. But it was my mother's wish. He was a nice man; he had all the money and he thought that was enough. He never read anything, never learned how to speak English correctly. My sister was the extreme opposite—she went to school and she read all the time and she became very discouraged with him. But nobody ever had a divorce; you didn't love your husband, you didn't love him.

My sister and my brother-in-law [came to pick me up in New York]. [In Chicago] I stayed at my sister's, of course. I spoke Russian; I spoke Polish; I knew the German language, and, well, that's a lot, but I didn't know English. I needed the help I got from her, and she was wonderful.

I was here only about two weeks and my sister took me to the opera. During intermission, I walked into the washroom, and a little girl that looked just like a Jewish girl came over and pinched me. She said, "I want to know if it's rouge or it's real color." And I looked at her and I already knew how to say, "Are you Jewish?" My God. It was just like I would have struck her with something. So I didn't tell my sister that right away; I thought it might hurt her 'cause I was hurt, you know. So a couple of weeks later when she asked me how I feel about this country, I said, "Oh, everybody seems wonderful, but there's still some bad people." She says, "You're not criticizing people because they don't speak correctly?" I says, "Oh no, no—that I understand," and I told her. She says, "Oh sure. We don't usually mingle with these types of people. Why should I seek out somebody Italian if she feels that way about me?"

I'd walk, everybody would smile at me, a little Russian girl with long hair and red cheeks. They'd look at me, and they'd start talking and I didn't know what they were saying and I was very unhappy. So, I was going to school right away when I came but it still didn't do any good 'cause I was in a group with foreign people. It was a night school for foreigners. They didn't have the desire that I had, so I told my teacher, "I don't think that I'm learning, 'cause you're so busy with everybody." So then he suggested I get somebody like a private tutor should come, and I said, "Anything. So long as I'll learn."

I did that, and I went to another school that was much better, and I wish I would have continued. When I was eighteen I met a young man, and before I knew, I was married—you know those things. Unfortunately when you're in a little city like I was brought up, you have no chance, nothing else happens. I could have continued to go to school; even at my age now I think about it, why didn't I? Because I could have done a lot of things—for children. I could have been teaching; I could have worked with boys.

I walked around with my little dictionary under my arm, and I read a lot, and I kept constantly searching for vocabulary. My sister lived in a very nice neighborhood, and the next-door neighbor said to me, "Oh, you ain't goin' to school today?" I looked at her and I came in and I told my sister, "These people are supposed to be Americans. What kind of a language do they speak?" And every time that somebody made an error, you know, I detected instantly, and my sister was so proud of me. I was so eager to learn how to handle the English language.

Then I decided that it would be best for me to get a job. I started to go to school right away at night; so I thought, "Why can't I go to school at night and work during the day?" And I did, all kinds of jobs, but it paid money. First of all, I took care of children.

Then I worked in a shop, sewing. I thought, "What have I got to lose? I know how to use a machine." [My family owned a machine in Russia], oh yes, sure, and I used to stitch and sew my brother' pants;

I think I started when I was five years old to fix up. I worked in that place for a long time, and I was the only girl who was from Russia, and the ladies that owned this place used to say to me, "Do you know, you speak more correctly than anybody here. How do you do it?" But my sister didn't want me to stay there. She said it's hard work. "You come home and you're tired," and it's true I worked very hard to prove that I can do everything.

Before I came to this country, since I was about fourteen, I was so crazy about this particular boy. We went to school together. But when I came here, it all ended. He really wanted to come, but I couldn't bring him. Well, you had to be married [to emigrate] in those days— or a brother or a sister. I didn't think I could ever really be in love with anybody else. That was the worst part about it all.

But the American boys didn't leave me alone. That's true, you know. I was different, because I had red cheeks and I didn't use rouge (that's all they used to talk about). My brother-in-law was very strict. He wouldn't let me walk alone.

I met him [my future husband] when I was here about a week and my brother-in-law didn't trust me to go home alone when I got out of school. I was going at night, and I came out and there was a boy waiting for me and he'd been doing it several nights already. When I saw him, I nearly dropped. But I saw everybody else being free. So he said to me, can he walk me home? So I said, "Well, you could except my brother-in-law is coming; I can't walk away." So as we were standing and talking, my brother-in-law came, and they looked at each other. My brother-in-law said to him, "What are you doing here?" And he said, "Well, I saw her and I thought maybe I can walk home with her." He says, "What's your name?" (First he wants to find out if he's Jewish.) Then he says, "I know your father!" Oh and the smile on his face because the father is that wonderful family, and they have a lot of money. And I got permission to see him. He was very handsome when you didn't know anything about him, and he spoke English and I didn't. I thought that was really something. We used to go out dancing, and all the girls used to look at him. But I started to speak English, and I detected that he didn't speak correctly—he was born in this country.

My brother-in-law pressured me very much. He was after me because he says, "The parents are very rich; he's gonna go in business with them and you'll have a good life, a happy life." If I marry him, my brother-in-law will be lucky. How can I ever refuse? After all, I was a young girl. But in my heart, I knew there was something. So it went on and on, and then he bought me a gorgeous ring and unfortunately I married him.

I didn't comprehend him really, the young man I married. I don't say he wasn't nice. He was four years older than I. People admired him. But I don't know, I started to expect more. What I believed in, he didn't. It's very hard, you can't live with a man like that. I think that's the worst thing in the world—when supposedly you're married, and you're supposed to be together. I don't say you always believe exactly, but at least if there's some understanding. I used to just look at him, and then finally we started to argue. I started feeling ashamed of him. I was happy when he kept his mouth shut, really.

My little boy was born, and he was mean to him. I think that brought it on more. [By the time] my little boy was five, all he did is walk in and eat. It's like living with a man in the house to just take care of him, cook for him, wash . . . in those days a woman worked very hard. I gave. That's all. Never got anything. Even a wife you can't expect everything. So I left him. And finally we got a divorce. The day came and we went to court, and he didn't show up, so simple as that.

My first husband—I would have loved it if he never bothered me. Oh, it's terrible to marry someone you don't love. Honest to God, whether the man has money, he doesn't have any money, but if you have love for him, that's the end, really and truly. You live with a man for possessions but you get so used to it, it means nothing to you. 'Cause I know many friends, they married this man because he was a successful lawyer; they married the doctor because he was doing so beautifully.

I have an older brother—moved in with me and we had a beautiful apartment; my brother paid rent. My sister'd come and just fill up the refrigerator so that we have good food, and we got along beautifully. My sister didn't want me to [work]; she wanted me to be with my little boy. She supported me. And one day, I went to the grocery store and there's a young man. I kind of admired him; he was a student at the University of Chicago, he had started to work on his master's. He'd carry my groceries for me and my little boy was crazy about him. He started to come evenings, and we used to go out and we'd take my little boy everywhere.

And my sister, brother-in-law: "You're still young, now is your chance"—you know how people talk. Grab somebody while you can. And I told my brother-in-law, "Yes, grab somebody like my first husband that you thought it was such a great idea. Nobody can grab me anymore. I have to be in love in order to marry. Money is nothing to me; if I'll be able to feed my child and have a roof over my head, then that's the kind of a life I want to lead."

So he called me, my boyfriend, one night and I said, "I don't think you care, and I can't go on like this. I want to have somebody to take care of my little boy instead of being just with me. If you'd love me, you'd marry me. We've been going like this for three years and I'm tired of being alone."

First thing in the morning the telephone rang. He says, "How would you like to get married today?" We didn't have a ceremony or anything. We just went to the judge, and that was the happiest day of my life. I was twenty-eight, and at least I started to read books and I understood life and people and that makes a difference. He was a very gentle man. He lived up to my expectations. He was a landscape architect and a husband to be proud of—educated. He was wonderful.

After nine months I had Diane and then Billie—two daughters. Very fast, and he wanted that. He says, "Might as well have a few kids. What's the use of waiting?" Neither one of us were youngsters; we were in our thirties. I would have loved another son.

[We moved around at first.] One time, we lived in South Bend, Indiana, in a little house, and next door to us lived a family. They weren't Jewish, I didn't know what they were, and I didn't even really care anymore. If they're nice, then who cares? So the first morning I walked out—we had a little yard—to put up a few things.
She had three children, this woman, and the little girls came out to the fence next to my yard, and they said, "Hi." And I said, "Hi, darling. How are you?" The mother came out and grabbed them and pushed them in the house and told them never to talk to me again: I was a Jew. The older boy heard all that, the son of theirs, felt so terrible, when she left for some reason with the little girls, he came out to me and he said, "I'm sorry my mother treated you like that." She was a simple, ordinary, ignorant woman and she was pregnant; she was going to have her fourth child.

Slowly, slowly she was getting sort of nicer. So one time she got sick, and I saw the children sort of lonely and forlorn. They didn't know what to do and she had to go to the doctor. So I thought, "What have I got to lose, I'll take a chance." I said, "Would you mind if I give the children lunch? You're going away." She looked and she says, "Oh, would you?" and I took them into the house. And she got home and she thanked me. Then she went to the hospital to have the baby; I tried to take care of the little girls, little boy.

When she came back, I made some soup and I brought it over and her parents were there. And I was just going to drop off the soup that I thought would be good for her and she says, "Come here, Mrs. Pollock, come here. I want you to meet my parents, who taught me the rotten stuff that you discovered when you moved here. And I've never known anyone so wonderful as you are."

I know I could have done many things. [After we moved back to Chicago,] my husband was gone all day, I used to look for something exciting. I invited the students to come to eat dinner with us. They worked for him. One time, I knew a man that owned a dress store, and he said, "Would you like to do a little work for me? Saleswoman, I could use one." The kids were at college. So I was selling. I liked it and I did beautifully. My husband made me stop. He said, "You're on your feet all day. What do you want to do that for? I can take care of you." But I really didn't want to, I'll never forget that. I knew everybody. They'd walk in and see me, they'd stand in line, wait for me. I guess he was jealous. Never wanted to let go of me, wanted to make sure I'm home and everything's fine. So whatever he said, I did. But the money came in handy; we were never rich, you know.

Then my son, aged twenty, was the most wonderful boy, went to the last war, came back, happy, healthy, beautiful, got a lovely girl, was going to get married,—and he got polio. It came in June; he died in August. I don't know; after my son died, I needed help; I needed something in this world to turn to. And the rabbi used to come to see me at least four, five nights a week. He said we must believe in something, we have to believe that there was a God, and everytime he talked to me, I was thinking about it. I'd cry every night; I would just stand there and look at the sky and cry 'cause my son died.

After that, the girls were away and my husband didn't let me work; there were a lot of people that I knew and I liked but I was never the type to just run around to lunches and fool around. Then suddenly I saw an ad in the paper about a housemother for boys; and I said to my husband, "You know, that's what I'd love to do. I'm so lonely and I miss my son so much that I feel that I could give something that they haven't got." So the next day we went to the school for boys. And I was there for six years. I didn't save any of my money when I was there because the kids like little snacks and there was nothing in the house. So I used to go there [to Chicago Heights] and bring snacks and little drinks and the kids had a wonderful time.

I was still there, and that day I don't know what happened. I'd been doing it for two years: we [my husband and I] kiss goodbye; we're all as gay as we can be, and that day was the end. He wouldn't let go of me, he was holding onto me. And the kids [at the school] were so happy to see me. I was sitting having dinner in the central dining room with the boys and I cried; I don't know why. Later we heard a knock on the door of the boys' cottage. And there were my two daughters with tears all over their faces. "Ma, it's Daddy." He dropped dead behind the door. So that was the end of my wonderful life. When he died, I had nothing, just myself to take care of myself. My husband never had life insurance. They wouldn't take him; he had high blood pressure.

After the birth of my grandson, I decided to get a job in the city. And I was here in Chicago for about four days and I saw an ad, a housemother. You live with the kids and you're with them all the time. In other words, you sort of take a mother's place, if you have it in your heart. I can love anybody's child, honest to God. I got the job. So I tried my very best; I've always felt if you're going to accept a job like that you have to have it in your heart and be a part of a mother or you have no right.

I had a stroke about seven years ago. I didn't know what happened to me. It was my day off, and I was sitting in the playground watching my grandson; and I felt so relaxed, and I thought, "My God, what's so wonderful about today?" and I started to walk and I couldn't. My grandson saved my life. He says, "Ma, where are you going? That's not going home." I said, "No, darling." I didn't want to tell him how I felt; so he held my hand, we came [home]. I lied down; my daughter called a doctor. He said, "I'll be over as soon as I can." Took him several hours, and he examined me and he says, "I have to take you to the hospital." I waited eight days to get to the hospital; they didn't have room. I didn't stay in bed; I got out and I walked, but I knew there was something wrong with me.

Finally I came to the hospital. Oh God, what I went through. Cuts all over me—you know, my arms. Try to dig in, see what really happened. They kept examining my head, my brain. I went through everything under the sun. I was there for five weeks. I wasn't sixty-five yet. I was paying for it. The school helped. But I kept walking and [would] shake suddenly. The doctor said, "There's a little bit of damage but it'll come back. Don't worry about a thing." And I think it did too. I'm just as wonderful as ever—ha, ha.

I really felt sorry for the kids, and I loved them; they were wonderful. But I felt since I had that happen to me, I may have another one and never recover. And it was all emotional connotations 'cause there's no work just sitting talking to the kids. But it was hard on me—might as well face it, eight kids in the house, and they all wanted to talk, and they all wanted help, so you sit with them and how can you say no? It was a little too much for me. When I left my job, I was already sixty-five years old. And I felt, "Well, I've got my Social Security. I'm taken care of." I thought it was a good idea. I would have stayed on if I would have felt more secure about my health.

I think kids keep you from getting senile. I love to read. I can just sit and read and read. Oh, my daughter needs me so I figure, well, I'll read at night, as much as I can, but I have to spend time with my grandchildren. Time marches on—before I know, I may not be able to.

When Rachel [my granddaughter] was little, I used to walk about twenty blocks one way and twenty blocks back with my little girl. I used to walk by the U of C [University of Chicago], and there were some professors and they'd stand there. "Wow, what a grandma, how do you do it?" I says, "The older, the better, you know." And when I got a little tired, I'd sit on some bench and everybody got to know me. I had a wonderful time; I was never alone. So it was good.

You know, now that I'm getting old I'm thinking of the little old ladies that I used to run out and talk to [in Russia] as a little girl. This particular little old lady— I never forgot her; it's a funny thing how you can think of a particular person. She was very old. She was a neighbor. And I'd come over and we'd sit and talk, and she would thank me, and I'd bring her the cherries in our backyard. I told the little old lady, if she can read books, I'll bring her some of mine, and she told me she can't see. She always used to cry. I never stopped thinking about her.

And I'm criticized by elderly women for constantly being with my granddaughter. I don't drag downtown with them to eat lunch. I can't see it. Then when I said I can't during the day, "All right, let's go to a movie at night." I can remember when I was reading a marvelous book, and I thought, "Oh my God, why do you want to go to a movie and sit there with this little old lady," that's all she thinks about.

Some of the elderly women, the way they talk about this and that and the boys with long hair—oooh. They got angry with me because one boy, a student from the university, came up and said hello to me. Sweet, friendly, I don't even know his name—but he saw me on the playground for years, sitting there with my grandchildren, you know. He says, "I looked all over and I didn't see you; I'm so glad you're here."

And now some silly people come up to me and ask why don't I get married? I'll be seventy-two years old. I'm old, but I'm young at heart. I understand people, and I love people, but it would have to be somebody I admire. Otherwise you marry a man just because he has a big beautiful house and $50,000 in the bank. So how can I marry someone like that? What'll I do with that? And I met him on the playground (this was last summer); he used to be a psychiatrist. He says, "I know you're probably about fifty from the way you carry on." He says, "I have a gorgeous home and I don't know how many thousands." I thought to myself, "If you had millions, I don't care what you have, that's not what I'd marry you for."

Oh my God, men like that, you marry them, they still want to sleep with you. He took my hand and I thought I'll die. And I thought that's what he wants to marry me for. So he'll sleep with me and I'll cook and I'll take care of him, so I'll have a "wonderful" life, what good is the money? No, really, it's ridiculous. Thank God, my children are taken care of. It ran through my mind many times, God forbid, my children starved and I'd have to do it to help them. But for myself, I have a beautiful little apartment—I love it. Nobody gives me a penny 'cause I don't need it.

So what I'm trying to bring out—sometimes elderly people they take all these things seriously and they do the wrong things instead of keeping up, just see what happens. You become frightened. I lived a long time already. When I retired, why should I start pampering myself? I thought I'll keep up and if anything happens, so I'll die. We have to go. Five years earlier—five years later. People tell me, ooh I don't look seventy-two. It's not the way I look. I look it. But it's the way I act.

Ida Richter: The Entrepreneur/Raconteur

Ida Richter's experiences not only epitomize those of the upwardly mobile businesswoman, but also portend some of the feminist changes of the 1970s. Her materialism, her keen business sense, her pride in success, her discontent with the traditional role of Jewish wife and mother reflect more of an accommodation with American culture than a rebellion against her Russian background. On the one hand, she has retained the charitable impulse, the emphasis on family, and the obligations of the dutiful daughter of the *shtetl*. On the other, she believes she has realized the immigrant's dream of upward mobility, of achieving a middle-class lifesytle and possessions.

She is also a storyteller who can hold you to your seat. In her old age, she turned from business to the writing of novels. Her first novel, *Echo of Tomorrow*, is an insightful story of an immigrant woman whose life somewhat parallels her own. Her second, *Compassion*, portrays life in twentieth-century Chicago and deals with such controversial topics as adultery, impotence, and miscegenation. Mrs. Richter has kindly consented to let us include excerpts from *Echo of Tomorrow* in her chapter, permitting us to attain an interplay between spontaneous remembrance and a view of the past created in fiction.

The ambition and determination which energized her in her youth and middle age still prompt and direct her life at eighty. To know her tells us that, for some, widowhood and old age are a challenge, not an ending.

Ida Richter

I DON'T THINK OF MY-
SELF AS A WRITER. I've read much better ones. I started
just to write like an autobiography for my grandchildren—how we
came to America, how we were on the ship. Just to get myself busy
and do something, to express myself and to get my thoughts from all
the things that happened, to spill it out. I didn't know how to write;
when I was younger, I didn't have the time and I didn't have the life.

I couldn't sleep nights, and I'm a very energetic person. So four
o'clock I used to start to write something. To write, you need an in
with different families, and different people, and I know them all.
I taught myself. I didn't even know what kind of name I'm going to
use, I just wrote. When somebody said, "It's a novel," I said, "Is it?"

My children and grandchildren all read it. "Keep on writing; please,
keep on writing." So I wrote. I had to spill out because when I used
to talk about when I was a child to my children, it was a different life
than they have; so my daughters used to say, "Mother, write! Why
don't you write it down? Nobody knows things like that."

Well, I was a very observant person. I used to be crazy about my
father, and he was a worldly man. Besides being a hard worker, he
was learned in the *Talmud*. And when I was a little girl, I used to sit
right near him; and they have discussions—how the Russian and
Japanese war was going on. And I used to observe it and also my
mother used to tell me about things [from] when she was a girl,
and I started to write it down.

On the long winter nights in Russia, as everyone huddled
around the large warm oven, Bessie told and retold the stories
of their family. Only Jennie remained awake to listen as the other
children often dozed and fell asleep one by one. But Jennie could
never hear enough, and always the pictures became more vivid
and alive as she grew older. . . . Bessie had grown up in a world

121

of fear, in which religion was the only refuge and hope. Under the
Russian government, the Jews suffered more than anyone else in
that country. During the reign of Czar Nikolai, army conscrip-
tions for Jewish boys started at the age of thirteen. If they were
not registered at birth, spies for the government would come into
the Jewish homes and catch these young boys. They would dress
the boys in long army coats that often hung to the floor, while
on their feet were strapped heavy high boots. During their twenty-five years of service, the young soldiers were taught the Greek
Orthodox religion; many never saw their parents again. My
mother cried in fear not only for her own sons but who would be
left for her daughters to marry?

My writing was very hard to read because I didn't have punctuation
or spelling or English or diction. I didn't go that far [in] school, and
I didn't care. I wrote how I knew, what I knew, the people I knew,
and what they had done. I put in a little bit more of my own thoughts.
A lot of people read the book and they say, "How do you remember?"
And I say, "I remember."

My parents had seven children, and we lived in White Russia. They
used to call it Russ-Poland, but there were Polish, Germans, Russians.[1]
My father was a blacksmith, and a carriage-maker in Kletsk. Nearest
city was Minsk, the capital.

We lived natural there. The life in Russia was a little more primitive,
more natural. How much my father made was enough because the
Gentiles used to bring us commodities, and my father worked for
them, repaired their wagons, and gave them little trinkets, and they
used to bring him food. They didn't have much money either. So it
was like barter. We had two cows. My mother had a vegetable garden
in the back of the house. When it was in season, we had plenty of
vegetables. From the cows, we made cheese and butter, and the children had enough milk. Most of the time, we ate rye bread and milk,
and I thought it's a terrible diet; now my children said that was the
best diet because the bread was made [of] natural rye and that's
really why we were healthy. For Sabbath, [it] had to be chicken or
meat and *kugel* or *kasheh*; and during the week, we had meat because
there were working people; my father worked hard. Meat came from
the *kosher* butcher in the middle of the town.

When it started to get cold there—the cold [stayed] there for three months—my father didn't have much work. The people didn't come in to repair the things; they used to have sleds. At best, we had food enough. Then, before their Easter, it started to get busy again. We survived on and off like that. He had help, a couple peasants; he had to pay the help whether we had work or not. They didn't get much, but you had to feed them. In those days, the help lived with you.

All the Jews lived in the *shtetl*; and the Gentiles lived [on the] out-skirts of town or on the farms. They used to call it a *dorf*. Because the peasants were all around, they used to come in town to do the buying and the selling. They used to make sandals from the bark of the trees. They used to make pots for cooking, earthen pots. And they used to bring in their livestock to us. Before their Easter used to be terrible market days. [So many] people used to come, they didn't have a place where to park the horses or the wagons. And we used to have busi-ness with them.

I don't remember how many families were in the *shtetl*. It must have been a couple thousand. There was a richer class. We weren't the poorest—we were right in the middle. It was quite a town; I'll tell you how it was situated. The marketplace was in the middle, and the streets started from the marketplace, maybe about ten streets.

We lived in a very unique street; it was a place where they used to go swimming, and it was canals on each side, trees on both sides, and the fields, corn, rye, and all kinds of vegetables. It was a very beautiful spot there. Only our street was like paved with cobblestones. The rest of the streets were all made of dirt. And across the street, we had a well that was good water. Some didn't even have that.

In each street was a synagogue because a Jew is not supposed to walk and carry things [on Sabbath or a holiday]. And then we had a Polish church and a Polish bank. But the Polish people didn't have much say there because Russia invaded Poland way back when, and the Polish people were treated just like the Jews.

The Russians had control. We had a *duma*, a city hall. And also on our end of our street was another government house that was like a little jail; they used to call this the *kantseliarskii*. You registered there, and they used to have there a cop. When people were caught in a different town, they used to walk to our town, and the guard used to ride on horses with daggers; or they used to catch him without a pass-port in a different town, they used to bring him back there to register.[2]

We built a house about ten years before we left. We weren't like the peasants; we were already a little bit modernized. Otherwise we had an old house with no floors. In fact, the old house they used to rent out, but the people never paid rent. They had a lot of children, the man didn't work, and whatever he made—the first time my parents saw a drunken Jew. Used to drink up the money what he had.[3]

[My father inherited the house] from my great grandfather. I'll tell you what happened. When my mother only had two or three children and life was very hard, my mother begged my father, "Let's go to America." He says, "How can I leave all this that's gonna be for me when my father dies?"

My mother was a beautiful woman. She was raised in between Gentiles on a *dorf*, and she spoke very good Russian, [though] they didn't socialize or visit each other because it wasn't right for a Jewish girl to be among Gentiles.

[My parents'] was an arranged marriage, and my mother comes from a better family; they were a rabbinical family from way back when. My mother had eleven children. Four died from epidemics: scarlet fever, diptheria. Two boys died within ten days; one was six, one was four. They were the first ones, and my mother was very upset. Sometimes there wasn't a doctor in the town, and even if there was a doctor, what could he do? One child got sick, they all got sick. Sometimes [there] were storms and the storm broke a window, and it was fifty and forty below zero. What could you do? They caught a cold, and then they were sick, and they died. Four children died. My mother was never the same.

> In our town, there was only one doctor, and a *hegdesch* instead of a hospital. This *hegdesch* was like a poor house. If a poor man was traveling and didn't have a place to stay, he slept there on the floor. Or a diseased person lay there till he died.

Oh, she had so much work, my poor mother. We had two cows; she had to feed them. There was a barn at the back of our house. And to wash clothes by the pond or in the house from nine or ten people —the people that worked for my father, she had to wash their clothes, too—and cook for them three meals a day. And before a holiday, we used to rejoice, and when I used to say to her, "We like holidays so," she said, "Not me; when a holiday used to come, I was tired before

it came. To do all the work for all the cooking for all the people."
My older sisters, they thought [they were] too good to do some housework. They have to be pretty for a *shiddach*. I was in the middle,
born 1895: "You don't need a new dress. You go do for me this and
you go do for me that, and you take care of the children." I was ten
years old, I used to chop this and do this for the house. I used to do a
little sewing, and I used to be right near my mother.

And that brother of mine, three years younger, was the most spoiled
brat ever until he died. When they made a cake or a compote, my
mother gave it to him. She used to give him coins he should eat. I
resented him. I was doing everything in the house. And he used to
walk around like a king and hit everybody, and it was fine because
he was a boy and we were girls. I wanted to show him I can be better
than him. [It made me] more aggressive, and more wanting to be
myself.

In Russia, a woman was nothing. [But a Jewish woman] when she
had a boy, she was the cream of the crop. A boy was a very important
thing in Jewish life for a lot of things. When my father used to pray
in the morning with his prayer shawl, I used to hear him say in Hebrew,
"Thank God I'm not a woman." A girl wasn't much.[4] When a boy
was born, they made him a *bris* and the rabbi came and the neighbors
came and they baked cakes and they washed the walls and they washed
the benches and the tables. Everybody was there dressed up. I remember when my brother Harry was born, I was three years old. I
ran out on the street and I watched the rabbi coming with the mink
collar.

My family was very Orthodox. We couldn't wait for the Sabbath
day, so we used to dress up Friday, wash our hair and put on a clean
dress; and the house was cleaned, the *challeh* was baked, the table
set, make the beds, and the chores for the next day was ready. And
those little Gentile children used to go to the government school. I
used to be so sorry for them, they haven't got a Sabbath like me.

On Sabbath, my parents went to synagogue and we would wait for
them. When the parents came back, we would sit together. My father
would take a nap and then he would sit down and read to us the
Payrich in Hebrew, but he translated in Yiddish: how to conduct yourself. And I used to sit and gob every word up.

Passover was the best holiday. We all got new clothes, new shoes, and we were washed and dressed, and the house was painted and cleaned. They started to work on it four weeks before, to scrub everything and change the dishes. We had to go to the pond to wash [them]. And we used to set the table with all colored glasses, and little wine glasses. We dressed up from morning until night, and we used to rejoice. And we used to go to synagogue.

Yom Kippur was a very sad holiday. My father and mother used to dress and put up a very high candle for the dead from long ago; and [one candle] for those nearest and dearest that died. They would dress in stockings like somebody died. They didn't wear shoes and they sat on benches. Young children didn't fast, but I wanted to.

For *Succoth*, my father used to build a beautiful *succoth* with windows and branches on the top because we had to look out to the stars, and benches there. That was at night, and then, during the day, guests used to come. The children had to be away from the guests because they talked politics and religion.

[We went to the synagogue and the women] sat upstairs.[5] Only once a year, at *Simchath Torah*, women can go down in the men's department and dance around the *Torah*. We were kids; we couldn't wait till that time had come. We used to kiss the *sepharim*, the scroll, and we used to march around it holding hands.

You know, one *Yom Kippur*, my parents were in the synagogue and a herd of Cossacks came on great big horses. [It was] the first time that I saw it in my life. They heard there's Revolutionists living in our town, and they started to go in parade with great big fur hats with open daggers. Well, we ran up [to] the attic; and there was a little window. We were afraid they're going to kill us. We were kids. We looked out the window [at] how they were; we were shuddering, and we only wished our parents shouldn't walk out from the synagogue now, they would kill them.

My parents knew what's up. They didn't talk too much about protesters or the government. They used to sigh in the synagogue: "God should only give us the strength. The enemy shouldn't find anything on us."

There were all kinds of [political] parties. There was the Zion-Labor parties, the Socialist Democratic Party, the Bund, the Socialist Party, the Anarchist Party.[6]

My father had a man working for him, a young man, Jewish. Somebody snitched on him that he's a leader in the youth. So the *zhandarm* came to look for this man and his name was Yankel. "Where's Yankel?" My mother knew. A night before, she dressed him up in women's clothes, and he laid on a roof in an attic across the street. But my mother had made some bread for the week, and she put it on the couch and covered it up with a tablecloth; and the police thought that the man was there. They went and grabbed it, so my mother thought: "He's going to take it away! We'll have no bread for the week." So she went before him to cover [it] with her body, like you can't take it. Well, he threw her across the floor and uncovered that, and the boy wasn't there. Anyhow, they took him in a covered wagon to the next city and put him on the train to Germany, and he waited for the ship to come to America. A Jew would help a Jew in anything because, if not, then who would help him?

So we didn't mingle with Gentile children, never; and we didn't go to a government school because one percent of Jews could go there, so who would go one percent between Gentile? So we would have a private teacher to come in the house couple times a week. They used to teach Russian, Hebrew, and Yiddish; and I was, I think, about five or six years old and I was too young. They didn't want to pay for me, but I observed what the teacher taught my sisters. I took a twig and a pen, tie it around with a string, and write the alphabet.

We had to leave for a lot of reasons. There started in fact the Revolution in 1905 in Russia. I had a brother, a Zionist; he was involved and they were looking for him, the government. Well, anyhow, my mother had three brothers here [who] came in 1880. So she sent him away to the brothers, and another sister came later. [Then my sister] sent a ticket and the next sister came. There was no life for the children in Russia because there was no schooling for the Jews. So my mother wrote to the children and her brothers that "we cannot live in Russia anymore; and there's no future for us. People that your father deals with feel that they're enemies to us." They didn't want to pay for the work my father done. So my father sold his shop and the house, and we started to come to America in 1907. I was twelve. Half the town left.

Well, my father couldn't get a passport because a son of his died when he was a little boy, six years, and they didn't erase him in the city hall. They thought that he too left for America, and they demanded

him for the army. They didn't believe he died. My father would have
to pay three hundred dollars, like a fine, or confiscate his business and
the house. So he went to the governor in Minsk to fill out an affidavit.
He was pickpocketed; they took away his money; three days he didn't
eat.

My father then didn't have enough money even to come to America.
So he had to go to an agent that used to give you a passport for about
fifty dollars—forged. On the depot, the guards were watching for
him; and they thought he had the money. But my father was smart. My
mother left with the money before; she put it in a pocket in her dress,
sewed it in, and she was waiting for us in Minsk to come make the
passport. It took a couple of weeks.

Anyhow, we missed the ship in the meantime. We had to wait a
couple of weeks for the ship to come in Libau—that's the port.

> Jennie stepped off the plank, following the steward down the
> narrow passageway to the third class quarters. The ship smelled
> of fresh paint. A crowd of people stood on deck waving and sing-
> ing revolutionist songs against Russia. . . .

> After three weeks on the ocean, the passengers were weary—
> nothing but sky and water around them. Tonight the waves are
> calm; the reflection of the full moon is like a strip of silver on
> the water. The long dream of so many of the immigrants would
> at last be fulfilled. All kinds of faces. All kinds of thoughts. . . .
> No one wants to sleep tonight; everyone wants to stay awake to
> catch the first glimpse of America. By morning, all were dressed
> in their best outfits; but still no sight of land. As they watched for
> the promised land, the immigrants tried to envision what their
> futures would hold.

When we came in Ellis Island, they had a law made; each person,
each child, should show they have enough money—twenty-five dollars
each. We were short seventy-five dollars for the three children to show,
and they wouldn't let us out till we [could] get the [money]. And my
father and mother were out of their minds. They thought they were
going to send us back. Just imagine—to go back with no shop and
no house, and the government is looking for you. And they were
crying. Two weeks, we were like in a jail; we had to live with such a
dirt and such a smells and such a terrible, terrible place.

After two weeks, from the HIAS came a nice-looking Jewish man
and he sent a telegram [to my brothers and sister], and in a couple
of hours, there was a telegram that the money is put for the children
there. And we finally came to Chicago.

> Oh America, we love you! And we love everyone here for being
> so wonderful, especially the five room flat upstairs of a store.
> . . . There were plenty of rolls and bread on the table; and a
> brand new toilet in the hall to be shared by two families. Not like
> in the Old Country without even a privy. We all had to go behind
> the fence.

We had two large beds in one room, two in each bed. It wasn't very
important for a child to have a room. You slept on the floor, on the
couch. I slept on a black couch near the stove. 'Course, I used to get
a headache once in a while from the gas fumes, but who cared? Everybody was so busy keeping alive.

A couch wasn't supposed to be empty. My mother once had an
empty couch, so she went to the grocery store and said, "If you know
somebody that wants to come and sleep, I got a couch." So they send
over a man; he had his wife in Russia, and he was a carpenter. He didn't
work, so whenever he had to pay, my mother said, "Forget about it."
So he used to buy a quarter chicken and put it in my mother's soup.
My mother used to give him his chicken and the soup and side dishes,
and that's how it was. She said, "A poor man; you got to give him
help."

When we first came, we were very happy. It was coming down to a
heaven, a haven; we lived very poorly in the ghetto, but it was better
than to be under the Russian government. We're happy to work, I'll
tell you. Those days, my mother was glad to live in a ghetto. She had
her friends, her language, she had her synagogue near the house. And
Saturday, the whole pleasure they had was to get washed, dressed,
on Sabbath, and go to *shul* and talk to the neighbors and listen to
the cantor and to the rabbi. That was their only pleasure.

We were more close than ever. After supper, my mother used to
buy a pack of apples and put this on the table, and we used to sit and
talk and tell stories and do some sewing and do some washing, and
we were together.

We used to visit my uncles and aunts, especially on Sabbath. I'll tell you, we looked up on the American cousins. They looked down upon us. After a while, we found out we were smarter than them for a lot of reasons. We used to say, "Oh, they don't know—American fools, their parents take care of them, and they don't know anything." They really didn't—they went to school, they were Jewish educated, they only knew their little circles; but we went to factories, to lectures, to meetings from the union.

We spoke English all the time outside of the house because my mother used to say, "This is a Yiddish house and no Gentile languages are going to be spoken here." That wasn't right. We used to love the American people, to copy them. I wanted to be an American very much. I saw people who looked better and dressed better and I wanted to be like that kind. Making money, too. I found out that you're something with money. My father used to say, "A person without money is like a dead man."

My father worked for my brother. He was a mechanic. He worked very cheap because he was old. There was a lot of people wanted a job like that, so my father was glad he had a job. But sometimes he used to cry when he was a big boss and now he had to work for somebody else.

And here in this country, this kind of working wasn't such a terrible thing because the people around us were all working people and very few had an education. In those days, if you graduated eighth grade, you were great.

Well, I started to go to school. It was the third or the fourth grade, I went a year and a half and my mother said—before the Passover, my younger brother broke a leg—"Have you got a heart to go to school when such a tragedy's happened? The house isn't *kosher*, and Harry broke a leg. You think you gonna run away from everything, from all the trouble. You better stay home." And since that time, I didn't go to school, [except] on and off. That time I didn't resent: the women were looked on those days like the weaker sex.

So I had to help my parents with washing, [had to] scrub out five rooms. And after six months, I says, "I can't work so hard. I have no money. I have no clothes, I have no shoes." My mother says, "Those that work need shoes and clothes, and spend the money." So I says, "Well, then, I'll go to work." So I had a job folding shorts, pants, overalls, packing them in boxes, standing at a high table, I hardly could reach it. Two and a half dollars a week, ten hours a day. I was fourteen. Beginning was very nice, just to get out of the house.

On and off, I worked in different places, for Jews mostly. We spoke English. I worked on a sewing machine. I used to [be] a sleevemaker.

And then I got a job downtown in a dress factory [working] for an Irishman. I worked there two years before I was married. We had to work ten hours a day for a little money. You had to be fast to make a living because they paid you for piecework.[7] They gave us a quarter a dress. A day, you had to make about eight. Two dollars a day was a lot of money. The conditions were terrible. Naturally in the summer, there was no air-conditioning; and the lint and the dust and the dirt and the smell. The toilet was like a little box.

> After a time, she grew very tired. The heat of summer made her feet swell. Her packing table was near the toilet room that was used by both men and women. It was a small room with no lighting facilities, and the smell was more than she could bear. She would often gaze out the window where she could see girls her age playing ball on the street. This made her very sad. She could hardly wait for the whistle to blow at 6:30 so she could go home.

I belonged, after a while, to the union. I had marriage in my mind so I didn't want to be an ardent member. I thought to myself: "I just want to work and get through and after a while, to get married." I was afraid to go out on strike.[8]

> There was some noise going on and a patrol wagon came near the sidewalk where all the people were standing. About six policemen jumped out. When Jennie saw this, she ran into a nearby hall and looked out the door window to see a policeman pick up his club. The other policemen followed. One woman spit at the officers as she was being dragged to the patrol wagon. Some women were screaming and one bit a policeman's hand. Some of the women walked to the wagon without any protest. After the noise had subsided, Jennie started for home. She had had a guilty feeling with the picketing of the day, the police and all that had taken place. She felt perhaps she should have gone with the women.

My mother said it was easier [in America] but life wasn't normal; the people weren't normal, everybody was in a hurry and money was the main thing in life and religion dropped, even in our house. I said you should do things, you should try to make a better living, a better house.

I made enough to take care of myself. I used to do my own clothes and I used to go out on dates. Wednesday and Saturday and Sunday were dating.

The girls [in the shop] used to talk about this one got married and this one got rich; even if she wasn't rich, she pretended she was. And we used to sit in the sweatshop and work and we used to think: "Oh, look at this one; she's much better off than I am." Another one says, "What, so what! She's got a husband; she has to scrub and clean and diapers and have the babies."

The main thing was in Jewish life that a girl should work a while and get married a nice, decent man; he should make a living. Education my mother didn't care for. She says, "An educated boy can't make a living. A boy that has got a trade is the best."

So my husband had a trade; he was a cutter on men's clothing. When I started to go out with my husband, I was eighteen years old. And after we were courting for six months, he gave me an engagement ring. It was very important in those days.

But we couldn't get married. He used to be on and off of work. There were strikes. Hart, Schaffner, Marx, 1910, had a strike for three months. He went out on strike; he was out of work the whole winter. That was hard times. Then he got a job, and we got married because I loved him. I married a very nice man, a good-looking man.

We got three rooms on top of a saloon. It was cheap. It was nine dollars a month.

> When she said she would take it, the owner asked her if she would like to bring her mother to look at it. "No," said Jennie, "that won't be necessary. This flat is for my husband and my-self." . . . As they ascended the stairs, Jennie could hear the echo of her own footsteps. The hallway was dirty and the marking of the walls showed that a large cross had been hanging there. Jennie noticed the sun coming through the opened windows. Fresh air blew in and she knew she could clean up this place and make it look beautiful.

My husband wouldn't go to parties. Everything stopped like, and I was very unhappy about it. But then we got into hard work and into saving money and thinking of the future. The times were bad, and people worried about it. I had two children, I'll tell you—I started to get smart, not to have so many children. My mother, after I was married six years and I only had two children, says "Oh, if I only knew what to do, I wouldn't have [had] twelve children."

I wanted to work, but my husband wouldn't allow me so we were always looking for a business. I pushed my husband to go in business. "You'll never amount to anything if you work for somebody else," and that was true. I was always beside my husband, always. He wasn't aggressive; I was more aggressive.

We opened up a little shop making children's clothes, so I worked in the shop; and he used to cut and I used to take care of the girls. My mother said a woman couldn't do that. You have enough, the house and the children. You do a better job with the children if you're not in business. But I did both. My younger daughter was nine months when I went to the shop, but I got a Jewish housekeeper on and off. I come home [and] sometimes I didn't know where the housekeeper was. I didn't feel good for the children's sake; I had a guilty feeling. But I was also happy to get out of the house and be between people, talk about business; that was my life.

Then my husband [became] partners in a small town in Clinton, Illinois. [We were] there five years because somebody had a factory there and they abandoned it. The Ku Klux Klan was very powerful in those days, 1923. And we used to have the KKK—three K's—on the sidewalk and on the door. I went through anti-Semitism so much here because we lived in a Gentile neighborhood. There were only five Jewish families, and they intermarried. I have seen the Gentile life. I lived with them—much different.

Well, I seen how my children felt. One time, they read a story "The Jew Among Thorns" in the textbook, and when [my daughter] went down to recess, they all pointed to her, she's a Jew, too. She said, "Mother, I felt so bad. Is it bad to be a Jew?" I told her, "It's nice to be a Jew. You're just as swell as everybody." She said, "But they looked so funny at me." And when it was *Yom Kippur* and we observed that holiday— that's the only holiday really we observed—she laid on the couch and she told her girlfriends she's sick; she didn't want to tell them that we have a Jewish holiday. Now is this a way to live for a Jew? That's why I told him, "We're going back to Chicago."

We came [back]. We started to go in real estate; we had some money
saved up. [Then] the Depression came in full swing. My husband lost
his money; the bank closed. So we scraped up a little money and we
had a little building, so we traded that for a meat market and grocery
on the near South Side. We stayed there thirteen years. I worked in
that store; I would [have liked] to have another baby, but I didn't
have any time. I went and I made potato salad and cole slaw, and used
to sell it fifteen cents a pound; and then we made sales, like a penny an
egg. And minced ham, twenty-five cents a pound. It was a Gentile
store. The people in that neighborhood had big families, and the women
used to go work nights [while] the men worked daytime. So they used
to come for breakfast five o'clock in the morning to buy. I used to get
up four o'clock, take two buses, and go to the store.

And then we bought our building back. Was thirteen apartments.
But we didn't sell the store. After a while, my husband got sick, and I
got sick—well, anyhow, we managed. He started to invest in real
estate again, and this is not a Russian life that I'm telling you because we
were like the middle class now. We used to collect money for the poor
to send to Europe. I was the President of the Ladies' Auxiliary, and
he was the President, Secretary, and Treasurer of a *verein*.

I'll tell you, at that time, if a person made a living and she had a
little better clothes than the average Jewish woman had, and she has
an apartment a little better than that, you consider yourself lucky. And
a man to look after you and to be with the children, with the family.
To work hard and make something. It was important. To get a nice
house, and nice clothes and better food and a better life for my children.
I cared for my parents; after a while, they got old, they couldn't work and
I had to work for them. And then his parents were in Europe; we had
to send them money. So we were happy to do what we can.

After we sold the grocery store, and I couldn't stand staying home
and I felt I'm losing money some way, I opened the dress store because
I was bored, I had to do something. My kids were in college. It was a
little store.

Well, anyhow, from one place to another, I found out I didn't have
much schooling, I better go to school. I went on and off, in night
school, day school.

After my husband passed away, I was left in a three-bedroom apartment alone. That was fourteen years ago.

Jennie couldn't believe it. People came and left and talked to Jennie, telling her life must go on without Alex now. Where there is life and strength, life does go on. . . . Jennie knew from now on I have to be strong and learn to live alone, not to be a burden to her children. . . . She knew she must not be afraid anymore because Alex was always near her. Sometimes she forgot that he was gone and called his name. At times, she could almost hear his footsteps. When she lay alone at night, she would plan her days ahead and would say to herself that whatever years God would give her, she would live it fully.

Now I sew, and I belong to the Senior Citizens' Center. When I was younger, I resented being old. My face changed, my body changed, my hair was getting gray. And now I'm very happy about being old. I have more understanding of the world. I see things with different eyes than when I was young. I was like in a daze, looking at things and not having my own ideas and waiting for somebody to tell me. I know now. I know what's all about.

Ruth Katz

Ruth Katz: The Loneliness of Old Age

Ruth Katz feels her life really started here in America, where she learned to be independent and self-assertive. When she arrived from Poland in 1913, she was forced to take care of her own affairs. This initial lesson in self-reliance served her well, even within her marriage. She is quite articulate about the status of women in Poland and America. Nevertheless, her struggle to become independent was undertaken not as a self-conscious feminist, but rather as a sixteen-year-old eager to take advantage of the opportunities of America.

Mrs. Katz, in some ways, summarizes many of the themes of this book. Her life in America illustrates the great aspirations immigrant women had for their children and the hard work involved in helping them realize such hopes. Her career in small business demonstrates that immigrants often had to start from scratch at least twice—upon arrival and after the Depression—and they had to establish businesses in what to them were alien and hostile neighborhoods. Her marriage was a partnership based on mutual love and respect rather than the more traditional bonds of her parents' relationship.

Mrs. Katz articulates the fear and depression many people feel in old age. They are faced with the loss of family and friends who shared solace and memories. They feel they can no longer contribute to a society which overvalues youth, independence, and productivity. In her struggle to maintain her dignity, she reminds us that the elderly are not merely "memory banks" but individuals who are still growing and experiencing even though they are perhaps now facing the most grueling and traumatic time of their lives.

L

ET ME TELL YOU
SOMETHING. I say we are the forgotten people. It isn't a blessing
to live long. You know, I may look outwardly happy-go-lucky and
in perfect health, but there's no such thing at the age of seventy-eight.
And recently—I lose my balance; it's a little frightening. And I never
write to my daughter my problems. Everyone has their own problems
—why should I burden her? She's so far away [in California.] My
granddaughter goes to work and writes her. My daughter got alarmed.
"Mother, I'm so worried; I'm so worried." I called her and I say,
"Honey, don't worry about Mother; Mother is perfectly all right. I
am an old woman and I pay a price for reaching my age. Your mother
has her own coffee pot hidden in my little place where I'm in nobody's
way. I don't have to ask anybody to support me. I can still get up in
the morning and make my own coffee and take care of myself during
the day. So you have nothing to worry . . ." I said to my daughter,
"Being old is not a blessing."

And I'm telling you the same thing. You go downstairs here [an
apartment building for the elderly], and you see how much the old
people suffer and how many children don't bother with the parents. And
what good is old age for?

I just lost a friend in here. If he lived he would have been eighty-two
years old—very fine man. We were very, very devoted friends. And I
broke my arm last year and while I was in the cast, he calls me up and
he says, "Ruth, I have to go into the hospital." I knew that three years
before he had surgery on his stomach [for cancer]; I didn't know it was
serious. I says, "Sol, what's wrong? Is it the old problem?" He says,
"Yes." So I says, "How about coming in? I'll make a cup of coffee
before you go." So with my one arm, I manage for myself, I make
coffee. When he was in the hospital, I called him practically every day,
cheered him up a little bit, and when he came back, I tried to be as

helpful as I could. I used to call him up, "Sol, what are you doing there
upstairs? Come down, we'll have a card game." But when he start[ed]
coming downstairs less, I realized that it's toward the end of Sol. He
was three weeks in pain. He had a daughter in California; she didn't
come out till after he died. He had a son here—was too busy to visit
the father. The last time I came up to see Sol, it upsetted me terrible
because I lost a sister from cancer and I lost my husband from cancer.
And I know what Sol was going through. What do you think
happened?

They came in and they found Sol on the floor. Unconscious—they
didn't know how long he lay there. This is the end of us—we're not
animals. I always say my husband was a very fortunate man; he had
me by his side all the time. God forbid something will happen to *me*.
It'll be tough. But let's not think of it. It's not that you regret that
you're getting old. It's the heartbreak that all that you have behind is
meaningless, and you're so very lonely.

What have you got at the end? Children have their own life; they
can't bother with old parents. How much time do you have for your
parents? You'll come in to say hello and maybe on a holiday have a
meal with them. Maybe once in a while, you'll take them to a movie. This
is all. You have your own life.

What have we got to offer? We don't contribute anymore. Who needs
my experience? Each one must work out his own problems. This is what
ripens us—[making] mistakes and paying for it. We can't live somebody's else's life and nobody can live our lives either. I firmly believe
not to bother the children—not interrupt the children's life.

You know, every night before I go to bed—I'm not religious— I say
a prayer of thanks for the blessings of the day, that I could go through
the day peacefully, and I say, "God dear, if my time is up, I should not
wake up." But we don't die when we want to die, and we don't have the
courage to finish it either. That takes an awful lot of courage.

Something else I'll tell you. I didn't know what old age meant. You
see, I wasn't home with my parents when they got old, so I didn't know
what old age meant till I moved in here. That opened my eyes. I go
up to the laundry. And I see a woman there—new face—and I says,
"You just moved in?" and she says, "Yes." I says, "What do you pay
for your apartment?" She says, "Two hundred dollars. What do I care?
I lived with my daughter. My daughter came here and rented the

apartment. She pays the rent." Do you see? The daughter wanted to get rid of the mother; she came and rented an apartment. She paid way above [the going rate], just to not have her around.

In Europe, family sticks together. There was no such thing as old people living alone. But I'm gonna tell you something that I remember my father saying. "Move in one room and be by yourself, because living with your children, you're bringing *sin* upon your children."

You know, my husband died, that was a big shock after forty-two years married. But my daughter lived in the same building; I had my grandchildren. Either I came [to my daughter's] or she'd come to my place. We used to go downtown. All of a sudden my son-in-law got a better position [in Boston], and they moved, a terrible shock. And then I gave up the business; I had that apartment building twenty-three years; everybody knew me and respected me, and I didn't know what to do, where to turn.

When I sold the building, I didn't think I'll remain in Chicago. I thought that I'll move to Boston. And I went to Boston and I looked around a little bit and I saw if I moved, I'll be a burden on my daughter. I wouldn't know how to get around myself. I would have to bother her taking me places; I would have no friends. So I came back, and I start looking for an apartment; and every time I went into a building I got the chills—to go and move somewhere where nobody knows me, I know no one. You know, it's not easy to break up everything that you worked for and strived for; and losing your partner of life is not easy. It's so lonely.

I was born in Poland. It was called Russ-Poland, [that part of Poland] had been taken over by the Russians. We felt the identification with the Jews, but we were more towards the Russians than towards the Polish. We used to read Russian books and the Russian papers used to come in, and the Polish—very little.

The name of the town is Wizajny; now Wizajny is in the state of Suvalk. My father's name was Rabbi Moshe Mendel Wizansky. The town was named after my father. He was a prominent man; even under the czar administration, my father took a prominent place. The main officer of that town, who was a friend of my father, decided to honor my father and named the town.

It's a real small town. We had a large river, and there was done quite a bit of fishery there, and all around that river was nothing but trees and beautiful flowers. And in winter when that river froze up, we were skating across the river where there was another little town. Everybody knew the rabbi and his family. If there was a wedding, or a *bris*, naturally we were invited.

[The Gentiles] were all little farmers. Not many wealthy Jews lived in our town either. The Gentiles were mostly those that owned the farms. And the Jews mostly owned little stores. [The Gentiles] were very friendly if they weren't provoked. We had a fire in the middle of the night, and my father's clothes burned up and then he couldn't even go to synagogue. The Gentile farmers brought us food, and they also got together and saw that my father got clothes to wear.

In 1905 there was a Kishinev *pogrom*.[1] Well, after that, the czar decided that it was good to have *pogroms* all over. So it came [when I was] about six years old an order to the Russian highest officer to make a *pogrom* in our town for Sunday. So about one in the morning, that officer himself risked his life. He knocked on the window and told my father to go to synagogue and call all the Jews together and tell them to hide in the cellar for 24 hours—that tomorrow morning, when the soldiers come to kill the Jews, they'll open the doors and they won't see anybody; they'll think the Jews left. Middle of the night, my father called the Jews together.[2] We were a town of maybe 150 families. Never will I forget that experience, that 24 hours in the cellar. There was no water, no toilet services, but we managed.

My mother happened to be the only child. When she was four, she got engaged to her cousin [my father]. So when my father was eighteen and my mother not quite seventeen, they were married. My mother told me that she had a beautiful voice to sing; after she was married, they wouldn't allow her to sing anymore [because] a woman is not supposed to sing and excite a man with her voice. You know, they had to shave her head the day before her marriage, and she said when they shaved off her hair (she must have had beautiful black hair), that she cried. She cried till she had to get ready to go to the *chuppah*.

When my father was seventeen, he became a rabbi. My mother's father sent him to different towns to study, and he became a rabbi of the town where they lived and he died there as a rabbi. He was honored; he was respected, he was the most educated [in the town]. In the later years, there was a court, but there was no judge, so the government sent him to school so he could become a judge. In the whole state of Suvalk, whenever there was a trial to settle an estate, my father took care of the books. At times it took him months.

You see, in one way they sent my father to get an education and become judge, and the other way Jews were restricted to go to school; there was a quota. Because we were five girls, I didn't get a chance to go to school—I was the baby of nine children. [My mother] wanted education [for us girls]. They used to bring in a young man to teach, and in a quiet way [in order to avoid arguments with my father] my mother used to put me in there too! My father, whenever he could get time enough, he taught me. Whatever education I have, it came through my father. He taught me arithmetic; he tried to teach me a little of the Bible.

The only thing my father got paid for is the necessities for observance of *Shabbes*.[3] You know, on Friday night when you say the prayer (*Kiddush*) over the wine, every Jew had to buy the wine from us. And the candles. And the yeast Thursday to make *challeh*; everybody baked *challeh* so those that didn't have stores of their own used to buy already the flour from us; and oil and coffee—maybe it's like a little grocery store. Ma and all of us sisters worked on it. We used to buy the wine, believe it or not, from Siberia. It came in wooden barrels.

We were very comfortable. We had a big house; we had a building of four apartments. We had three apartments rented out. It was a nice brick building. Our apartment was a big one because we were a big family. Tell you one thing—[we] didn't have money. I remember that my mother used to say, "Five girls—we have to give them a dowry; where will I get the money?" But we never missed food or clothes.

[We had] inherited a "factory." Just one man and his wife took care of the factory. In part of the building was a big, flat rock, and then there was one, standing up sideways. We had a horse—you tied up his eyes that he shouldn't see the seeds we made oil from—und he was going round and around and around, till it was smashed. You heat up these seeds, and then you put them in sacks, and had them pressed out. It was delicious oil [for cooking]. You know what I used to love? After the seeds were broken down, you put the rye bread on top—ooh that was delicious—I liked the *taste* in my mouth. [The seeds] made like a cake or a bread; that was a big industry in our town for the German people because Germany didn't have anything like it and that was the best feed for cattle. So every Tuesday, market day, our house was full of German buyers, and they admired my father. They wouldn't do a thing without consulting my father. So he was a busy man in his way.

My mother was the boss. [She ran the factory and the store.] Oh
yes, she had time for everything. She never consulted my father on anything. She managed the whole affair. She raised the children. The only
time my father raised the children, if we woke up early in winter, he used
to dress us, and give us breakfast; and he used to bring a glass of milk
to my mother's bed. I tell you, inasmuch as I loved my father, inasmuch
as I respected, he made a mistake: for one thing he couldn't charge for
any rabbinical service (he said a rabbi doesn't sell a service); the second
thing, he was so absorbed in his duties as a rabbi that he neglected us
children. If my mother wouldn't be a bright woman, I wouldn't be able
to read and write more than Jewish. My father had a room and all the
walls were nothing but shelves and books. The kids run in, you know,
a little bit violent: "That's not a place for kids." My mother used to say,
"No, this *is* a place for kids; they have to learn." And he wouldn't say
another word.

My mother saw that every one of us children were assigned duties in
the house. There was no such thing, "I can't, Mother; I won't do it."
"This is your duty; if you want to eat, you've got to contribute." We had
ovens, and in the winter the ovens were supposed to heat up the whole
house, so in summer we used to buy like bricks from the farmers. I was
the one that had to go and see that the farmer doesn't cheat.

My father was home except if there was some business affair to settle.
[He] studied. And our house was always full of people, from our town
or visitors. My mother used to sit next to my father and watch the inci-
dents that used to occur. And she'd say do this way or that way, and he
listened. My father, in all the fifty years that he was rabbi, never issued a
divorce to a Gentile nor a Jewish. He used to say to them, "Today, I am
very busy, would you come Tuesday?" If they came Tuesday, "I am still
very busy, would you come Thursday?" And when they came Thursday, "Now you don't expect me to issue a divorce before *Shabbes*!"

[Several of my sisters] had an arranged marriage. When they were
young, they were beautiful. I think beauty meant a lot. My father used
to go to the *yeshiva* and pick the boys that he thought would be most
suitable. [He didn't use a matchmaker,] but I know there was in town a
matchmaker, because he used to wear a long cloak, and always walk
with an umbrella. You had to pay the groom, a thousand dollars was
the minimum. [Take, for example, my cousin;] they had a thousand
rubles put away for her dowry and she took that thousand rubles and

gave it to her brother to study; she never got married because she
didn't have the money, so she sacrificed her whole life.

My brother was a very choosy man; he didn't like the girl that my
father had chosen for him. So, the marriage was from a matchmaker.
After they decided that it's a good match, my mother went to that town
to see if she's a good housekeeper. A good wife was a good cook; she
went to *mikveh*, and she had children. [If she was a bad housekeeper,]
ah, then she was talked about. Then she [my brother's prospective
bride] came for two weeks to our house, and then he went there for a
holiday and got acquainted with that family. They got married.

One little incident I remember. My older sister gave birth to a child,
and she died three weeks after the child was born. So my parents and
us raised him. So he [my sister's husband] remarried and left for America. We never heard from him, till accidentally my sister met him on
the streetcar. It wasn't that he was mean. It was circumstances. You see,
he claims that he never forgot my sister. He always loved her, but he
had to remarry. You know, the Bible says that a man must be married
one month after the wife dies. They call it *sheloshim*; you mourn thirty
days.[4] Let's be very frank. I guess a woman has more control over her
sexual feelings than a man. I guess that must have been the reason.

An old maid was the worst thing that could happen [in Europe].
For the simple reason that [a woman] had to take a back seat. They
didn't allow a woman to get an education. The woman was only born
to be a mother and a housekeeper. They didn't think that a woman
is a human being. That's why it was so much harder. You know, we had
a well in the back of our building, and you had to fetch the water from
the well and bring it into the kitchen. So my brother wanted to do it for
us girls and my mother used to say, not for a rabbi's son, but it was all
right for the rabbi's daughters.

My father was very religious, but he wasn't very fanatic. You know,
in Europe you're not supposed to talk to a young man, or take a walk,
God forbid. But we had young men coming into our house, and my
father never mentioned a word. My mother wasn't that fanatic [either].
We had one room, we used to sit, the girls, and the boys would speak
to us, and on Friday nights, danced—this sister of mine had a most
beautiful voice—sing, and we had good times. In fact, I have a cousin
who was a boyfriend of mine. [But] when you have four older sisters
and you're only sixteen, you don't think of marriage. You know, in
Europe at fifteen, sixteen, you're a child yet, pushed around. In fact,

when I left for America I promised my mother that I will not get married before my sisters.

This country was entirely different. Though, when I was young, an old maid here wasn't the most pleasant thing to be either. Now a woman is so independent and she is self-supporting. I was a very lively person, and I always had boys after me.

Now there is a story about how I came to America [when] I was a little over sixteen years. We had a neighbor in Russia and he paid the soldiers that let boys [draftees] cross the border. So he was caught and he was sent to jail. My father went to the state and vouched for him and told them that he'll never do that business again if they'll free him. So that neighbor had a brother in Baltimore, who brought the whole family to Baltimore. And they wanted to be grateful to my father. They got a synagogue and they sent a contract for the whole family to come to Baltimore. Who wouldn't want to go to America? It was the most fascinating word—America. We thought nothing but America is paved with gold. Everybody in Europe thought that in those days—that the streets were paved with gold and you dressed beautifully. You didn't have to work.

But my mother said that she will not leave unless she sells everything; and she was particular whom she wanted to sell, that [might] take a little time. So that neighbor wrote, "Send me the two younger girls first. And by the time you'll sell, they'll go to school and get a little English education." So an older sister and I came to Baltimore.

It was a terrible boat. [We went] lower class. And my parents gave us enough food to take along, we should't have to eat *trayf* food. It took us twenty-one days.

When the boat reached Baltimore, the girlfriends of the girl of the people that I came to, they all came to look at the greenhorns; and one asked me to see my stockings. She wanted to know if greenhorns wear stockings with all different colors, and I wore black stockings.

I was very lonely, very homesick, and I got sick. And the doctor advised that either I go back or else [go to] a sister here in America (she was also married to a rabbi, in Chicago). So she took us to Chicago. I wasn't in Baltimore very long—maybe about two months. That was in 1913, and in 1914 we had the war. After the war, my parents were too. old and too broken up and too sick to come. The rest of the family never came. There were three girls and two brothers here.

I guess [my father] did [worry about sending us to America], but he didn't show it if he did. He knew that he's sending us to people that will really take care of us. It turned out different and I'm not sorry, because it made independent people out of my sister and me. I had to provide for myself for today and for tomorrow. I had to find a way of being independent. It's conditions that pulls you into it. When you know that you have to pay rent, and you have to support yourself, that in itself makes an independent person out of you. If somebody shelters you, you depend upon someone.

[In Chicago] we met a woman that came from the same town [as we did in Russia]. She was the most wonderful person. On a Friday night, she invited us to have dinner with her. So one Friday, it was slippery. It was December, and my sister and I walked there to have dinner. My sister fell, and [her] appendix busted. She was very, very sick for about six to eight months. She was in and out of the hospital, but I had to work and make enough to cover a little bit of the hospital and support myself. And do you know how much I was getting in a week? Five dollars! *And that was good.* Some people got three or four dollars.

In those days there were a lot of fancy bows and collars; I worked on that. A very nice guy I worked for—he was a German Jew, I think. Then I thought maybe if I'll change jobs, I'll make a little bit more. I went in and applied to work by machines and that was by the dozen [piecework]. Men wore garters and suspenders. Seven cents a dozen. I worked and made ten dollars or twelve dollars or fifteen dollars a week. On work there was no limit. I used to come in early in the morning and work to six, seven o'clock.

As soon as I got a job, I rented a room with a family. That was practically a basement apartment; a Jewish family had four rooms—a husband and wife, boy and girl. So one bedroom they used. The other bedroom they had for rent. I rented it for four dollars a month. I told them I had a sick sister in the hospital, and when she comes out she had to share the room with me—"so it'll cost you five dollars." I didn't cook. You could get for twenty cents a good dinner in a restaurant. So about three times a week I used to go out. The rest I used to buy smoked fish, cheese, cream, lox.

I met my husband after I was a year here. To begin with, we used to go out, the four of us. My sister and I, and his brother and him. We bought a nickel ice cream cone; for twenty-five cents we went to Jackson Park and you took a boat for an hour. There wasn't such a thing as going out for dinner; they went home, we went home. On weekdays, we didn't even go. Sometimes, when you were more serious with a girl, you took her out Wednesday for a movie—for ten cents you went to the movies; for ten cents you went into the ice cream parlor and you had an ice cream soda. *Who* was chaperoned? Not in this country. But no sex; I tell you I was five years going with my husband, and we never mentioned that word sex.

I got married, I was in my twenties. Not for the money—he couldn't give me anything. The boys weren't prepared to support us; they also came from Europe, unprepared. You just got married at that time. In this country I think all my generation got married for love. You think it's love, but when you're married for a while, life settles down more serious. It's not what you dreamt, but we make the best of it. One good thing about it is you get companionship. I know I went through a lot of surgery, and no one would do more for a wife than my husband did. When I was in the hospital, he neglected the business and everything. He was right there with me, and that's what it means, companionship. If you look for something else, there is no excitement in marriage. You both got to work both ways. You've got to meet him halfway. You must, regardless how modern we are. I must tell you one thing; a man's ego gets hurt very easily, and to have a halfway happy marriage, you must feed your husband's ego. I can only tell you from my own experience. You take me, I worked with my husband. We worked together, we slept together, we ate together, and that is *not* the best recipe for a happy marriage.

I always stood up for my rights as a wife. You know, too much togetherness, the novelty is worn off, and there was a lot of friction to begin with. When we got into the ladies' and children's line, naturally it was me more than my husband. If a woman came in and she wanted a foundation garment, she wouldn't approach my husband, or even a dress, she preferred me. My husband's feelings got hurt very much. One incident really changed our life to the better. On a Saturday night I was almost busted from busyness; every customer that my husband approached [said], "We'll wait for Ruth." When we closed the door, my husband made a terrible remark, and he was so worked up. I didn't say a word. I walked out and I took the bus and I went home. In the morning (my husband all the years that we were married made breakfast), he came up to me and he says, "Won't you come to the table?"

I says, "On one condition; that we sit down and we talk things over." I
says, "I'm your wife, and your partner, and I'm also your business associate." (We had a girl, Celia was her name.) "You talk with respect to
Celia. This is what I expect of you, and if you can't do it, we might as
well break up right today, but I will not stand for another insult or out-
burst of temper. Now otherwise I don't go to the store with you." So he
says, "How can we do it any other way?" And I said, "You cannot wait
on customers, because it's women's work. But you want to be active.
Fine, I need you. You take care of the books, the finance, and the stock
buying, and selling will be mine." You know, that was the best thing.
There was hardly friction between us; he didn't mix with mine, and I
didn't mix with him. Otherwise I don't think I could go through forty-
two years working together.

Whatever I have, we both worked for, both of us, and my husband
always valued my opinion. He never done anything without consulting
me. Every marriage has a lot of adjustments, and mine wasn't any different. My husband bathed my daughter till she was three months old,
and he washed diapers (you know, in those days, you washed diapers
by hand), and he washed the dinner dishes and the china. As a whole,
it was a good partnership.

I'm grateful I was married. I don't know if you call it pleasure; I
would call it satisfaction of life. [The kind] you get out of family life,
nothing else satisfies you that much. There is something when you have
a family—the hopes, the things that you want to do for them. Then
when they get married and they leave you, it's a sad time in life but still
you know that there is somebody in the world that cares for you. It's
just a wonderful feeling to become a mother. And much more wonderful is when you become a grandmother.

I'll never forget. My husband and I were in the hospital when my
granddaughter was delivered, and the doctor knew me. So the first
thing, he said to the nurse, "Before you bathe the baby, take it out to
the grandparents." And you know, with me, I still swear when the
nurse brought Barbara, Barbara looked at us; they say a newborn
baby doesn't see, but I swear that she looked at us. That was a
wonderful feeling.

At the time I came [to America], the woman was home cooking and
cleaning and raising the children. Women weren't supposed to go out
and work. In fact, during the Depression when we lost everything, when

my husband couldn't get a job, I went out and I got a job selling dresses.
I came back and I told him that I'm going to work tomorrow and he
says, "Not as long as I live." He wouldn't let me go. That was a disgrace.
That I think we brought from Europe, that a Jewish wife should not go
to work.

I would advise it to any woman: don't become a housewife only. It's
good to be a good housewife. But you got to have outside interests to
stimulate you. You'll become stale before the time. I don't think I'm
stale yet. My husband considered me aggressive and so does my daughter. I don't know if it's typical, it's circumstances. You know, when you
have a child, you want the child to get the best education, and if I would
sit still, and must sit in the house, I could never reach it. Only through
my aggressiveness, I am protected now.

You see there were good times in business and bad times, especially
the years that you begin with. I had so many different businesses. To
begin with, we had nothing to start with. My husband didn't have at
that time a trade that he could go back to work. He used to pick up
odd jobs, so I said to my husband, "I'll work and you work, and whatever we can, we'll arrange a life." I took care of a little candy store,
lived back of one room. If I wouldn't be aggressive, you couldn't do
that. That little candy store that I took care of paid my rent. The only
thing that I didn't like working is, when I lived in the back of the store,
my company were rats, that I was afraid of.

In the three months after I was married, I became already pregnant
and the room was cold. I stayed there for seven months. I sold the
store for $500. Then I thought that with $500 I was a rich woman.
$500! I took a little apartment, and I had my daughter and raised her
in the back of the business—selling bakery goods—and when my daughter was ten weeks old, my husband bought a little delicatessen, and I
lived in the back. This is the honest truth; my husband used to go to
the market, and buy a barrel of apples and I used to keep my daughter
on one hand and dip the apples in taffy with the other—sold them a
penny an apple. Ten cents a corned beef sandwich and they used to say,
"Put a little bit more corned beef on." So my daughter was about three
years old and I had a little cigar store and I also lived in the back and
my husband used to go out and do *any* kind of a job. Then [one of my
friends] had a department store. She thought that the neighborhood,
it was Lithuanian and German, is not good for her children; especially

no young man wanted to come out to that neighborhood to take the youngest daughter out and bring her back in the evening. So she said to me, "Look, this place will be good for you. You'll make friends and make a nice living." But it was hard to bring a little girl seven years to that neighborhood. I said. "Hannah, if I'll succeed as a mother, I'll succeed there. And if I'll fail, I'll fail anywheres." We wanted that store, and I had a friend whom I met at that factory where I was making the garters, and we remained friends. She came in one afternoon for a newspaper and I told her; the next day I found in the mail a check of $200 from her (and I felt some people are the most wonderful people and you don't know what a help it can be.) When I told my husband about it, he said, "I have a brother in New York. I will ask him if he can help us," and he got $500. We started a department store and in one year we had merchandise of $18,000. We really did tremendous.

I had mostly my customers Gentiles. There was always respect. I was never insulted as a Jew and neither was my husband, because I would never cheat, I would never take advantage. I was brought up to be honest and considerate and helpful. To understand if there are less fortunate people, you've got to help them, if you are more fortunate. That's the values that my parents gave me, and if you take something that doesn't belong to you, I know I'm not going to be punished by God, but I'll be punished by my conscience.

So we were doing very well and the Depression came along. We got wiped out again. We had to start from scratch. We couldn't start that big so we opened a little children's shop on Twenty-sixth near Kedzie. Then gradually I took in ladies' apparel too. And that was going very well till I took sick; I couldn't work. Then I was at the hospital and my husband came to see me and he said he's liquidating the business. I said, "Who kills the goose that lays the golden egg?" and he said he'd rather be a poor man here than a rich man on the cemetery. He sold it. Then we bought a little real estate so I didn't have to work, and my husband took care of the apartment.

One thing, I am very happy that whatever I did, I made friends. I made friends with my customers. When I was in the hospital, my daughter says, "The door doesn't close. Everybody opens the door to find out how you are." Then the real estate that I sold, I also made many friends. They still come to visit me. That means something, because I didn't treat them like they're tenants or my customers. I treated them like a human being. If they asked me for something, I used to tell them, "It's your home and if I possibly can do it I will. But lose money I cannot afford." And they were not just tenants to me. When we had bought the building, there was an old Jewish family who had an invalid daughter. She must have been even in her forties and was in a wheel-chair, and they had one daughter that had a nervous breakdown several times, and the old mother and father. So who could raise their rent? We never raised their rent. You have to be human. You know, a lot of people, if they wouldn't be human, I don't think I would survive.

I think that I contributed to this country quite a bit. I felt that I'm just as good as any American. Because when I came here, what was Chicago? What was this country? If you read history, you know what, I don't have to tell you, and I contributed a lot helping it develop. God knows what difficulty I had financially and I never went for any help.

Afterword: For the Record

Too often in the past, memoirs have been mined for facts rather than for their emotional content. Yet in these accounts, not only do the women describe how daily life was lived decades ago, but they also tell us how they see themselves. Their accounts are less an attempt to document the historical facts of a bygone way of life than an attempt to present its emotional tone. In recounting their lives, the women unfold the development of both their cultural values and their self-images.

These women have a completeness of vision lacked by younger women, for they have lived through most of the stages of a woman's life: childhood, girlhood, working, marriage, childbearing, motherhood, grandmotherhood. They have lived through most of the crises too: divorce, abortion, widowhood, the deaths of loved ones. As women, they view as central those experiences which men may see as peripheral: getting married, becoming a parent. They may have shared a commonality of experience with the men of their generation, but, as women, they carried an additional burden of restricted opportunities and limited expectations for women that men did not share.

As immigrants, they had the strength and flexibility to cope with the traumas of a new country and language. Those most likely to immigrate were often the least traditional and most rebellious, qualities which enabled them to break with their Old World life. Their adulthood, marriage, and old age in America were not those for which their upbringing had prepared them. Living conditions, personal mores, job possibilities, adherence to religious traditions—all shifted suddenly, as soon as they boarded the ships to come here.

Part of the initial trauma of immigration involved reconciling two different cultures. These immigrant women came to this country already socialized into the East European Jewish culture; as a result, there was never the possibility that they could become one hundred percent American. Although they may have absorbed American ways, they still adhered in part to an East European Jewish mode of acting and viewing the world. In particular, they retained a clear sense of their Jewish identity. They remained rooted in their old culture even though some may feel they have fully adapted to the new one.

Too often, immigrants have been considered mere receptacles for "wonderful" American notions. These women, like all immigrants, gave to their new society as well as took from it. They actively reconciled the old with the new, and through this process, they changed America in subtle ways. For example, when Jews began to arrive from Eastern Europe in the 1870s, the American woman was unlikely to be working; yet by the crest of the immigration wave, immigrant women had not only made the working woman an enduring part of the social fabric, but they had also helped to organize the unions which gave working people job security. Because of the poverty of their material circumstances, these immigrant women were forced to become independent; and they in turn transmitted the benefits of their struggle to Americans.

If we have succeeded at all in this book, we have shown that stereotypes do not adequately describe reality. No one image of the immigrant woman can be formulated. We have said that stereotypes have no character. By our use of oral history, we hope these accounts do have character. Even in old age, when they might be tired by years of struggle and change, none of these women seems as lifeless as the stereotypes. They all have their hopes, their dreams, their disillusionments, their crises, which continue to change as they continue to grow.

The women of this book were carefully selected from a larger group whom we met through word-of-mouth, friends, rabbis, and social workers in the Hyde Park and East Rogers Park area of Chicago. We chose to work in Chicago not only because we live there but also because it seemed to us that immigrant histories usually tend to accentuate those people whose experiences were centrally in New York. We felt the book would have additional value if it were centered around those who had settled in an urban environment which had not provoked much analysis.

We interviewed the women approximately four to eight hours each, using an open-ended technique which we felt would encourage them to talk freely. The interviews themselves were informal. We presented ourselves as young Jewish women interested in hearing about and recording the experiences of women old enough to be our grandmothers.

We sought out women who were articulate and coherent, and who could describe the events of their past vividly. We chose them from as wide a spectrum of experience as possible, so that the most diverse lives would be represented in some way. We were unable to interview single, childless, or professional women, or women whose journey to this country took them through the Far East. Nevertheless, we feel the accounts we have included flow together to form a portrait of a generation's experience.

Perhaps now is the time to admit that we were surprised by what these women told us. We too were under the influence of stereotypes. To a certain extent, we expected this generation to be rigid, provincial, and petit bourgeois. We had forgotten the excitement and drama of their lives as they left one culture and adjusted to another. We forgot too, in the self-centered manner of the young, that ours is not the only generation that has agonized over decisions, hurried to seize opportunities we felt our parents ignored, struggled to become independent women, left our families, and refused to stop working and marry for security.

These women were born into and grew up during a tumultuous period of history: war and revolution, prejudice and violence were frequently daily occurrences in their lives. In many cases, they identified with what they considered the more modern elements of their changing society in Eastern Europe. They were more insistent upon acquiring an education and having the freedom to choose a husband than their parents or, in some cases, even their older sisters. Most of them rebelled against religious orthodoxy. Once in America, some were willing to forgo the traditional stability of Jewish family life to divorce a husband if a marriage turned out unhappily. Some opened small businesses as a way of directing their energy and drive into socially approved outlets.

Perhaps what we admired most about these women, however, was their spirit of daring and adventure. At most points in their lives, they were willing to take risks, to sacrifice stability for higher goals: freedom, education, love, material success. They rebelled against traditional notions of femininity and demanded equality in their marriages as well as the right to have a career and an education.

Their children, however, felt the differences between their parents and native American parents very strongly; to a certain extent, they were ashamed of their immigrant backgrounds. The children may have interpreted their parents' struggle for a better life as solely material. All they saw was the struggle itself and not the values which prompted it nor the goals toward which it was directed, many of which had been achieved merely by becoming part of American society. For example, while their parents may have seen education as a goal in itself, their children tended to see it as a step on the road to material success. When the Depression occurred, for the parents it was yet another crisis they would get through; for the children, it was a catalyst for their desire for stability and material security.

The grandchildren, though, may have an affinity with their grandparents that parent and child cannot share. Like our grandparents, we tend to think of ourselves as rebels. We like to feel, as they do, that we have left our parents and their outdated culture far behind. We do not, however, have our grandparents' endurance or bravery, not having taken their risks nor equalled their successes.

Whether we are grandchildren or not, if we open our ears to listen, perhaps the women of this book can speak to us of a commonality. Perhaps we can recognize in their struggles, our own; in their feelings, our feelings; in their lives, our lives. We can say to them, by listening, that they have given us something unique. We must tell them before it is too late that we have heard the message, grasped the meaning of their long lives, and taken them into our own.

Background Notes on Customs and Events

FANNIE SHAPIRO (*pseudonym*)

1. Portions of the 1881 May Laws prevented Jews from owning farm land. To circumvent them, Jews often rented land or paid a Gentile to hold title for them.

2. "Peasant language" refers to Belorussian, the language of White Russia. Mrs. Shapiro contrasts it to the literary and standard Russian used in novels and by the well-educated, and to "her own language," Yiddish.

3. To be *kosher*, meat had to be taken from certain parts of a "clean" and healthy animal (no pork, shellfish, etc.) killed by a ritual slaughterer, the *shochet*. The slaughtering had to be done as mercifully as possible—in one blow with a sharp knife by a trained man. Then the housewife would drain the blood by "*koshering*," that is, by salting and by rinsing. Due to taxes on *kosher* meat levied by the czar and/or the Jewish community, Jews paid more for their meat than the peasants.

4. As the climax of the week, the Sabbath required extensive preparations. No matter how the family ate during the week, the Sabbath meal was supposed to be a special one. Likewise, the home was specially cleaned, and everyone dressed in holiday clothes.

5. Crucial to the preparation of *kosher* meals is the separation of milk and meat products. Separate cooking and serving dishes must be used for milk and for meat, and a specified amount of time must separate the eating of each. Many common foods (eggs, fruit, vegetables, fish) fit into a third neutral category which can be combined with either.

6. *Bentsh licht* is the Yiddish term for the blessing over the Sabbath or festival candles, said by the women of the family. The candles are lit at sundown, the evening before the day of the holiday and symbolize the beginning of celebration. As she says the prayer in Hebrew, the woman may gesture as though embracing the candles, and cry. Afterward, she might pray in Yiddish for the family. Lighting candles and going to *mikveh* were two of the few commandments specifically for women.

7. *Mikveh* is the ritual bath married women were required to take after menstruation and childbirth before resuming sexual intercourse. Seven days after menstruation, women went to the bathhouse for purification in "the pool of 'living water' " (the actual washing had been done at home). During menstruation, a wife could not touch or even hand things directly to her husband, or indeed, to any man, unless the man was thoroughly purified afterward.

8. Immigrant husbands who sent back divorces instead of tickets were a major problem. Abraham Cahan's novel *Yekl* deals with the attraction the Americanized Jewish women held for Russian-Jewish greenhorns. Dr. David

Blaustein, the Harvard-educated Russian immigrant head of a settlement house, said of these greenhorn husbands: "He finds her [his newly immigrated wife] not five years behind him, but two centuries. He has acquired a new language, new clothes and customs, and a new country" (in *Portal to America*, edited by Allon Schoener).

9. A dowry, a *nadan*, was essential for a *shiddach*, an arranged marriage. The dowry was the daughter's equivalent of the parents' investment in the son's education. It would hopefully obtain a marriage with an educated boy of a family distinguished for its scholarship and charity, and would ensure security and children. A big enough dowry would compensate for any physical defect or could "buy" a scholar for an ignoramus family wishing to improve its "pedigree."

10. Mrs. Shapiro's parents were not eager for her to become a servant partly due to the low status of that job, particularly for unmarried women. Usually servants were peasants or poor married women.

11. Oscar Handlin's *The Uprooted*, a sketch of European immigrants' experiences in coming to America, emphasizes the stages in the trauma of transplanation. There was no chance to adjust to the myriad of new experiences. Between the decision to leave the Old Country and the confusion of the port cities, steerage, dealing with immigration officials, and finding a job and a place to stay, there was hardly any time to accustom oneself to the new way of life. Here, then, in Mrs. Shapiro's stream of associations can be seen the fusion of all the shocks that accompanied the act of emigration—the ship, Hamburg, being met at the gate in New York, etc.

12. The old man was easily recognizeable to her as a Galitzianer because of the type of Yiddish he spoke.

13. No, the banana is not a Freudian symbol here. Russian immigrants of all ages and both sexes were amazed and repelled by their first encounter with what was to them a strange tropical fruit. Not till after the 1870s was the banana common in the United States; its importation was partly due to the Banana Baron, Sam Zemurray, a Russian Jew who was a competitor of United Fruit.

14. The beards, earlocks, long caftan, and ritual garments of a religious male were part of the distinctive features which set off the Jew from the Gentile. Part of Americanization was the discarding of these distinguishing marks, required in Russia by ritual law and the desire to be set off from peasant neighbors; in America where they felt they could be accepted by Gentile Americans, many young Jews were willing to sacrifice religion to do so. Dress and shaving were the first habits to change.

15. Despite Mrs. Shapiro's disappointment, a candy store was an important institution in the ghetto, especially since owning a business was preferable to holding a job. A candy store actually sold much more than candy and could serve as an ice cream parlor or a clubhouse for boys.

16. *Grueneheim*, the Yiddish word for greenhorn, symbolized the confusion and alienation which affected all recent immigrants and the condescension with which they were treated.

17. The New York *Jewish Daily Forward* became the most widely read and most famous American Yiddish newspaper. Its most celebrated editor was Abraham Cahan, a Russian immigrant known as a Socialist. Not only did Cahan interpret America to his readers with articles on science and history, and a problem-solving column, "Bintel Brief," but he also interpreted the new immigrants to the American public in his short stories and novels and in his friendships with various reformers and men of letters like Jacob Riis and William Dean Howells.

18. The International Ladies Garment Workers Union (ILGWU) organized thousands of workers in this period. The strikes mentioned probably were the 1907 reefmakers' strike and the 1910 shirtwaist-makers' strike that took 20,000 workers out of work; most of the strikers in 1910 were women under 25, and the strike was known for attempts to recruit skeptical Italian workers.

19. She refers to the education and prestige ranking of the religious Jews in Eastern Europe. If a boy had talent and a family had the resources, the career chosen for him was always that of *Talmudic* scholar. Such a scholar would be able to arrange a marriage with a wealthy girl and would be supported all or most of his life by his father-in-law or working wife so he could spend all his time studying; even an artisan or laborer would try to approach the ideal by spending his spare time studying or by encouraging his son to do so.

SARAH ROTHMAN (*pseudonym*)

1. Following the spirit of social justice of the *Torah*, it was not uncommon for *rabbis* to sacrifice rigor in order to help the needy.

2. Stories of draft evasion under czarist rule are common because the Jewish soldiers were subject to anti-Semitism and obstacles to religious observation. Many draftees emigrated to America or mutilated themselves to avoid the draft. Even so, 400,000 Jews from the Russian empire served with the Russian army in World War I.

3. Very religious Jews associated the Russian language with peasants, anti-Semites, ungodly learning, and Christianity and disapproved of all Russian elements—food, politics, clothing.

4. Many Jewish women were illiterate, particularly within the generation of these women's parents. They had to depend on someone like Mrs. Rothman's mother to have prayers read to them in *shul*. If they could read, it was usually only in Yiddish; there was limited material available in Yiddish at that time. Paradoxically, because women were not expected to get a religious education, it was very often easier for them to acquire a secular education than for men.

5. A *Hasid* is a member of a separate Orthodox sect which is more mystical than the traditional orthodoxy. The sect originated as a rebellion against that orthodoxy and, in their less organized, more spontaneous, method of prayer, encouraged the involvement of Jews who could not obtain much education.

6. Eating bread on *Pesach* would be gossiped about since *matzoh* is to be

substituted for bread during Passover to commemorate the exodus from Egypt. All products associated with leavening should be removed from the house and a special set of dishes, untainted with leavening, used.

7. By 1917, there were 300,000 Zionists among the over 5 million Jews in the Russian empire. Ostensibly, people joined the Zionist Party because of an interest in promoting Palestine as a Jewish homeland. But there were few forms of entertainment or clubs for young Jewish people, and some joined the Zionists because they desired social activity. A good number of Russian and Polish Jews did go to Palestine in several waves; they founded the first *kibbutzim* and formed the nucleus of the first generation of Israel's leaders.

8. A great number of Jews rejoiced at the fall of the czarist government. Many had been involved in various secret movements and had supported important Jewish figures like Trotsky, Liber, Martov, and Zinoviev. Appropriately, on the first day of Passover, March 11, 1917, the provisional government terminated all anti-Semitic laws.

9. Jewish law forbade marriage between in-laws, step-kin, and siblings, and permitted marriage between first cousins or with one's niece or a deceased brother's wife. Marrying a relative solved the problem of dowry and of finding a spouse from a family of appropriate status.

10. Psalms often were read as prayers by family during the agonizing suspense of childbirth or sickness.

11. It was a belief in Europe that swaddling a baby made its bones straight, kept it from masturbating, and kept it warm. As the baby grew older, the swaddling was made less tight. The custom involved removing the swaddling several times a day so the baby could move around.

12. Balachowicz led anti-Semitic "volunteer" units who fought alongside the Poles in the Ukraine. Denikin was the head of the White Army from 1919 on, and despite his statements, promoted the tradition of anti-Semitism as a means of downgrading the unpopular policies of the non–anti-Semitic Soviets. Kolchak was a leader of one of the White Armies and became Commander-in-Chief and Supreme Ruler of Siberia for twelve months during the civil war.

13. Seats in the synagogue were bought to raise money for the *shul*. The most prestigious seats were those nearest the eastern wall where, facing Jerusalem, the *Torah* is kept.

14. The English woman's suffrage movement began seriously in the 1860s and was led by Mrs. Emmeline Pankhurst. Great publicity was generated in 1903 by the imprisonment of two leaders; in 1906 there was additional publicity when several women, arrested for protest activities, staged a hunger strike in prison. Note that Mrs. Rothman uses suffragist, preferred as a less condescending term than suffragette.

15. For a family such as Mrs. Rothman's, boarders were a way of life. They not only helped pay the rent but also might work in the landlord's sweatshop if he had a sub-contract for garment work. Very often, new immigrants experienced their first American home as boarders with friends, former neighbors, or relatives.

ROSE SOSKIN

1. During the nineteenth century, cities of the Pale experienced a huge increase in their Jewish population. Most of the new urban workers were artisans employed in small "factories" for as many as eighteen hours a day. Working under poor conditions, they earned only three to eight rubles a week. Jews were often in the weaving trades, but at this time, they also moved into the new cigarette, hosiery, tanning, bristle, and match industries.

2. Apparently, it was too expensive to keep an oven going constantly. However, since cooking on the Sabbath was forbidden, precooking had a higher priority than saving wood.

3. Galveston, Texas, may seem a strange entry point into the United States from Europe, but, for some years, it was the headquarters of the Jewish Immigrants Information Bureau. This organization, founded in 1906, was interested in breaking down the concentration of Jews on the East Coast and dispersing them to other parts of the country. While six thousand Jewish immigrants entered America through New York monthly, three hundred a month came through Galveston.

4. The letters HIAS stand for the Hebrew Sheltering and Immigrant Aid Society which opened in 1909. Gradually it had branches in several port cities and elsewhere. The Society checked on steerage conditions and cases of threatened deportation and served as advocate for immigrants. It took care of newly arrived immigrants and helped them get through Ellis Island and find their families and jobs. It also helped members of families stranded in Europe by the war. It sent representatives as soon as possible after the war to assess the situation and try to set up procedures to help relatives immigrate.

5. It was expected that daughters would marry in order of birth. Mrs. Soskin married out of the proper birth order, as she was not the oldest daughter. If there were many daughters in a family, there was special pressure upon the parents to match and marry off the older ones quickly and then find sufficient funds for the dowries of the younger girls.

6. Part of a marriage agreement was the *kest*—the right of the couple to live with the bride's family after marriage, especially if the groom were a Hebrew scholar who would thereby be able to continue his studies while his wife's family supported him.

7. The West Side of Chicago was at one time the ghetto for Jewish immigrants and was comparable to New York City's Lower East Side. In the era of heavy immigration, Yiddish was heard at least as frequently as English. The ghetto centered around Maxwell and Jefferson streets, and was complete with tenements, street markets, settlement houses such as Hull House, and Yiddish theater and intellectual cafes. Immigrants also formed their own clubs for self-improvement and educational purposes as well as for friendship and perpetuating old ties. Gradually, as the Jewish immigrant became better established, he or she moved out of the ghetto defined by Halsted and Polk or Halsted and Stewart and went south to Woodlawn, near Hyde Park, or further north and west.

The Jews who came in great numbers from the 1880s on were quite different from the Jews who had emigrated earlier; the later immigrants spoke Yiddish, dressed traditionally, kept more to themselves, and were not necessarily grateful for the patronizing kind of charity they received from the established Jews. By about 1900, out of a total population of 1,600,000 in Chicago, there were 75,000 Jews, of whom 50,000 were Russian. By 1926, Chicago had the third largest Jewish community in the world, exceeded by only New York City and Warsaw.

8. The Amalgamated Clothing Workers Union, which represented makers of men's clothing, began in Chicago.

9. The beaches of Lake Michigan form one edge of the city of Chicago.

10. The Sabbath was supposed to be the day of rest, of turning away from daily cares to God. To keep it so, extremely detailed rules of behavior were set up, based on interpretation of biblical regulations made in the Talmud and other rabbinical commentaries. For a family religious enough to have foregone non-*kosher* food during the wartime famine, it must have been extremely difficult to adjust to the necessity of having to work on Saturdays.

11. A *verein* was an organization of people from the same area in the Old Country. Immigrants often became so homesick that they were eager to renew old ties. The *vereins* held dances, organized charity drives, and occasionally formed a *shul*.

12. The Jewish People's Institute (the JPI) is something of a cross between a Jewish community center and a settlement house.

PEARL MOSCOWITZ (*pseudonym*)

1. The ideal husband for the daughter of a man who could afford the dowry was a scholar who had excelled in his years at the *yeshiva*. Among traditional East European Jews the male's key to social mobility and prestige was the application of a good mind to *Talmudic* studies.

2. *Trakhoma* is trachoma, an eye disease caused by a virus and transmitted by eye secretions upon contact with, or shared use of, for example, a towel. Trachoma affects the conjunctiva and cornea and can cause blindness through corneal scarring. Although Mrs. Moscowitz was told she had trachoma, her symptoms and aftereffects do not fit the usual description of the disease.

3. The agency which helped Mrs. Moscowitz's father secure land was probably the Jewish Agricultural and Industrial Aid Society, funded by the Baron de Hirsch Fund and established in Chicago in 1913. It was associated with the movement to prevent the flooding of American cities by Jewish immigrants. It made no charge for its help and only charged 5 percent interest on loans. Established German Jews were eager to get Russian Jews to enter the country through Galveston so they would not settle in the East and would spread out onto the land. Some of the utopian agricultural colonies established were in South Dakota, New Mexico, and Louisiana and were soon

defunct. Colonies in New Jersey and the Catskills survived by becoming resorts when farming was not successful. The South Haven area in Michigan, in which Mrs. Moscowitz's family became situated, likewise became a region to which Chicago Jews could escape the humidity of the city and was close enough to the city to make truck farming profitable.

KATYA GOVSKY (*pseudonym*)

1. Although the Jewish community was socially isolated from Russian peasants and the gentry, and often from the intelligentsia, within it, there was stratification and even sharp conflict. Class lines divided those who worked with their hands from those who worked with their heads. Some towns emphasized the distinctions through clothing restrictions and separate synagogues. Choice in marriage often made these distinctions evident.

2. Yeketerinoslav, now called Dnepropetrovsk, has a population of 660,000 and is a major city of the Ukraine. It is not surprising that several of the women in this book are from the Ukraine as, in 1917, sixty percent of Russian Jews lived there. In fact, in 1897, Yeketerinoslav itself was over 36 percent Jewish.

3. Merchants in Russia, until 1917, had their own legal class and were divided into two guilds. Membership was compulsory and expensive.

4. The Russian nobility preferred the French language to Russian to demonstrate its sophistication and cosmopolitanism. The small, wealthy Jewish upper class, separated by a wall of anti-Semitism, nevertheless copied the nobility; a few had sufficient wealth to buy acceptance. The Jewish upper crust was not defined by wealth alone, however. Family pedigree, *yichus*, and proper use of wealth were also important. One earned praise not just by giving money to the poor, but by donating funds in such a way as to "beautify" the recipient —to deemphasize the shame of receiving charity and downplay the plight of the poor. The poor, in their turn, offered the rich obedience, deference, and honor.

5. Every East European Jewish community had a network of charitable organizations which clothed and fed the needy, tended the sick, buried the dead, educated the poor and orphaned, and married off those women who could not afford dowries. Charity was an important value for East European Jews. Wealth per se was not admired, but what it could supply or make possible was: comforts, community service, and especially philanthropy. The reciprocity of the gift was not important. The emphasis was placed upon the donor's joy in sharing his good fortune and in receiving the recognition of God and the community for fulfilling the commandment to help others. Prosperity, however, was not necessary to philanthropy. Even a peddler woman barely able to provide for her son's education would give alms to a beggar on Friday, the eve of the Sabbath. Even age was immaterial: children might go door-to-door to collect contributions to help a friend or act as intermediaries to minimize the shame of taking charity.

6. *Pogroms* were riots tacitly sanctioned by the government and directed against the Jews. The first widespread *pogroms* occurred following the assassination of Alexander II in 1881. They occurred in over two hundred cities and towns. Some of the more infamous were Kishinev in 1903 (45 dead, 586 wounded), Odessa in 1905 (300 dead, thousands hurt), and Bialystok in 1906. The first major *pogrom* of this period, Kishinev, outraged public opinion outside Russia, and Jews in New York and Chicago organized relief funds and public demonstrations. The *pogroms* were responsible for swelling immigration from Russia, and most immigrants came to the United States.

7. The reference here is to the blood-ritual libel which served as the provocation for various *pogroms*. It was claimed that the blood of a Gentile child was needed to make *matzoh*, and on the basis of an accusation of such a ritual murder, a case was constructed against Mendel Beilis in Kiev in 1913. It is the case on which Bernard Malamud based *The Fixer*.

8. Jews in the Ukraine suffered greatly from the disruption of the civil war of 1917–1921, which followed the Revolution. There was a continuous changeover of ruling armies, most of whom were anti-Semitic. The Ukrainian army was led by Petlyura while the White Army, which included Cossacks and Russian officers, was under the leadership of Denikin. The White Army alone was responsible for 213 *pogroms*. There were independent bands led by Makhno and Grigoriyev, and "volunteers" under Balachowicz-Bulak, who were allied with the Poles. Only the Red Army did not have a policy of anti-Semitism, and hence the Bolsheviks were often welcomed by the Jews. It has been estimated that, during these years, there were over one thousand Jewish victims.

9. Although she does not allude to it, this was undoubtedly Mrs. Govsky's first shower. Almost unheard of in Europe, showers were popularized in this country by settlement houses which set them up to encourage American notions of hygiene among the immigrants.

10. The countries through which the hordes of immigrants passed on their way to North America feared epidemics. Hence Mrs. Govsky's frequent references to sterilization of clothing, medical checkups, and quarantines. The United States did not permit people with "contagious" or "loathsome" diseases, or those with obvious physical or mental defects to enter. Therefore, immigrants were examined for these, both before departure from Europe and before entry into this country.

11. By the time Mrs. Govsky's family left Russia, the new quota system resulting from the 1921 and 1924 immigration acts was in effect. Even before the quota system was established, the immigrant could not arrive simply and unofficially in the United States. Instead, the immigrant had to be checked by officials of the Federal Immigration Bureau, for example, at Ellis Island in New York City. Immigrants were examined by inspectors who had great discretionary powers. Although no money was legally required as guarantee for entrance, they could have immigrants deported for tuberculosis, trachoma, old age or youthfulness, poverty, and the absence of relatives to meet them. Any immigrant who entered this country through New York City had to pass

through Ellis Island. First and second-class passengers were rarely stopped.

12. Hyde Park is a neighborhood on the South Side of Chicago, where the University of Chicago is located.

13. In order to obtain a Jewish divorce, one of the marital partners must petition the rabbinical court to decide if and on what terms one partner must give or receive a *get*—a bill of divorce. Non-coerced consent of both partners is sufficient grounds. Contrary to some notions of Jewish divorce, the wife can initiate procedures if, as in this case, the husband refuses conjugal rights and support by his absence. The husband is supposed to write, sign, and deliver the *get*, after it is witnessed, to his wife. Then the wife gives the *get* to the court which in turn gives her a document asserting the legality of the divorce. A woman may not remarry for three months to establish paternity in case of pregnancy. A father can claim custody of any son over six years old.

ANUTA SHARROW

1. Such a trip by river was not uncommon due to the late development of Russian transportation. The Dneper, the third longest river in Europe, is known and still used for hydroelectric power, irrigation, and navigation.

2. Mrs. Sharrow's acceptance of this term for her father suggests that her family was more upper class than her designation of "middle" would indicate.

3. References to pianos in works of Sholom Aleichem and Abraham Cahan suggest that for many Jews a piano represented aristocracy.

4. *Gymnaziia* was the Russian version of secondary school and covered seven or eight years. In 1871, a government decree established a Jewish quota in such schools. Bribes, tuition, and living expenses were quite expensive, so Jews who were not wealthy rarely gained acceptance. There were two types of *gymnaziia*: classical and scientific. Apparently, few Russians attended either. According to the 1897 census the literacy rate among men in Russia was only 33.7 percent and among women an even lower 11.7 percent.

5. Leonid Andreyev (1871–1919) was a Russian author of short stories, essays, and plays sympathetic to the revolutionary movement.

6. Lenin spent much of his pre-revolutionary career in exile in Europe, particularly in Switzerland. Madame Krupskaya, his wife, shared in his work and was a leading ideologist for the Russian women's movement. She, like other revolutionary women, wrote revolutionary pamphlets.

7. Nikolai Vilatevich Lissenko (1842–1912) was a Ukrainian composer nicknamed the "little Russian nightingale." He studied with Rimsky-Korsakov, and fed the Ukrainian nationalist movement with his compositions. Lissenko is known for transforming various works of Gogol into operas. He established a music and drama school in opposition to the Imperial Russian Musical Society in Kiev, whose methods he considered sterile.

8. An *externi* studied on his own in order to attain a secondary school degree. To get the degree he had to pass an exam called the *attestat zrelosti*,

the functional equivalent to the French baccalaureate, and the prerequisite for entrance to a university.

9. The mission to which Mrs. Sharrow's husband was attached at the peace conference probably lost its credentials because of the confused state of Ukrainian politics. Lenin had supported an autonomous Ukraine partly out of political weakness. Although the Bolsheviks realized the value of its mineral wealth and huge wheat crop, they were not able to control it. After the February Revolution in 1917, Hrushevsky, Vinnichenko, and Petlyura emerged as nationalist leaders who set up a soviet and a government semi-independent of both the Bolsheviks and the central Russian government. With Petlyura as military secretary and Vinnichenko as prime minister, they tolerated the White Russian army, and received French support for their declaration of a Ukrainian Republic in 1917 (recognized at Brest-Litovsk). In 1918 and 1919, Kiev was alternately occupied by the Soviet armies (February 1918), the Rada armies of Petlyura (November 1918), the German armies associated with the Ukrainian puppet Skoropadsky (April-November 1918), and the Soviets again (February 1919). Because of guerrilla bands, remnants of German troops, French troops, Denikin's volunteer army, and a Polish invasion of Kiev, the Ukraine was not under firm Bolshevik control until 1921. In fact, Kiev was so much in dispute, it was possible for Petlyura and Skoropadsky to stage *pogroms* in 1919.

10. Humboldt Park is a section of Chicago on its northwest side where many immigrant Jews lived upon arrival.

MOLLIE LINKER

1. *Deutschland* refers to Lawndale, bordered by Kedzie and Douglas Park Boulevard, an area further north than the ghetto. It was called Deutschland because the Jews who moved there were thought to be taking after the Reform German Jews by becoming less traditional.

2. High fifth refers to the fact that grades used to be divided into half years. Promotion was not from one grade to another but from the lower to the upper half of one grade or from the upper half of one grade to the lower of the next.

3. Mary Antin was a Russian Jewish immigrant whose bestselling book, *The Promised Land* (1912), told of her family's life in Russia and her emigration to this country. It was popular because it described how the process of immigration made her into a very patriotic American, eager to give up her religious and cultural background.

4. To be able to attend High Holiday services it is often necessary to buy entrance tickets.

BEATRICE POLLOCK

1. There seems to have been much movement in and out of Russia by immigrants. Three of the women we interviewed had fathers who had come to the United States and then returned to Russia, while a fourth had a fiancé and a fifth had a brother who came back.

2. Among the Jews in Russia, doctors and lawyers were a sort of aristocracy. It was extremely difficult, as well as expensive, for Jews to get professional training because of the quota system legalized by the czarist government.

3. Among Orthodox Jews, abortion is as much a sin as avoidance of conception and childbearing, since it is the married couple's responsibility to reproduce and raise a family. Abortion may not be undertaken except to save the life of the mother. Mrs. Pollock's mother must have felt her role as childbearer more strongly than the fear of death.

4. The evil stepmother was a common cultural stereotype among the Jews in Russia. Remarriage was not unusual because of the high death rate in childbirth and because of the injunction especially placed upon men to remarry. Indeed, it was a functional necessity if a man was left with a large family and felt unable to cope with domestic responsibilities for which he was never trained.

IDA RICHTER

1. For many years "Poland" did not exist per se due to three partitions by Russia, Austria, and Prussia in 1772, 1793, and 1795. Only after World War I did an independent Poland re-emerge. In the first partition in 1772, Russia received Polish Livonia and White Russia. Then, after 1831, Russia formally gained so-called Congress Poland, which after 1815 had been semi-autonomous. Thus, Russia controlled at one time approximately three-quarters of the original Poland. Whenever one of the women refers to Poland, then, the date of reference must be kept in mind, as Poland's borders have changed several times since World War I, too. Besides, the woman might be referring to a political or ethnic Poland and not necessarily to a geographically recognized state.

2. The movement of Jews in Russia was restricted and passports necessary to travel between cities.

3. Drunkenness was almost unheard of among Jews in Europe, and Jews in America are still said to have a lower-than-average rate of alcoholism. Great distinctions were drawn by Jews between their own sobriety and what they saw as the frequent inebriation of the peasants. Alcohol was respected, since the Sabbath and holidays were sanctified through the blessing said over wine. Only on two days of the year were Jews "given" free rein with alcohol: on *Purim* and *Simchath Torah*.

4. The status of women among the East European Jews was ambiguous. A daily morning prayer for men thanks God for not making them women. The

female equivalent only thanks God for making women according to His will. Women were not required to participate in public religious ritual or engage in religious study. Girls were not honored at birth as were boys with a *bris*; nor was there a ceremony equivalent to *bar mitzvah* for girls. On the other hand, men were encouraged to marry and to treat their wives well, to give them financial, sexual, and emotional consideration as well as respect their competence in their own sphere, domestic work.

5. Religious and traditional Jews emphasized separation of the sexes in order to keep men focused on prayer and study, not sex. Thus sexes sat separately at *shul*, and at all times each sex was supposed to dress and act decorously. Early marriage was encouraged so that sexual interest could be channeled into a proper time and place, when it would be the responsibility of husband and wife to satisfy each other in frequent sexual intercourse.

6. Although political parties were illegal prior to 1905, many were organized and functioned effectively. The Social Democrats had representatives in all the *dumas*, the representative assemblies, while the Social Revolutionists, peasant-oriented, terrorist and anti-Semitic, had representatives in the second *Duma*. The Marxist Russian Social Democratic Workers Party, oriented toward the workers, divided into Lenin's Bolshevik faction and the Menshevik faction. The anarchists also divided, according to the philosopher followed— either Tolstoy, Bakunin, or Kropotkin. All but the followers of Tolstoy were terrorists. The Bund was the party of the Jewish workers, affiliated with the Social Democrats—they felt they needed a separate organization. The Bund was socialist and antagonistic to the Zionists because they advocated abandoning Russia for Palestine.

7. Piecework involved payment for each item of work the laborer completed; it was a substitute for the hourly wage. It favored the fast workers, if they could get all the bundles of work they wanted. In 1913 such a skilled worker might make $9 to $15 a week for sixty hours.

8. Most immigrant women saw their work as a temporary activity before marriage. Outside the garment trade, women were hardly organized at all and received lower wages than men, at times not even a living wage. They worked in terrible conditions, often at the mercy of a lecherous foreman or an unjust supervisor. Although marriage was fraught with the risk of an unfaithful or improvident husband who, if disabled or killed, could leave a woman with children to raise on her own, it seemed like a release to a young woman slaving in a sweatshop.

RUTH KATZ

1. See Note 6, Mrs. Govsky.

2. This story illustrates an important role expected of community leaders —that of *shtadlan*, or intercessor, a man who, by wealth or education, was given respect and privileges by the community and was expected to intercede

with the Gentiles in case of danger. He was to risk his life if necessary.

3. Strict and conscientious *rabbis* did not like to be paid for their services. They would cite the examples of famous *rabbis* in the past, such as the Baal Shem Tov or Hillel, who preferred to support themselves through manual labor so they could give their knowledge without charging for it. A compromise often used in Eastern Europe was to give the *rabbi*'s family the monopoly sale on certain essential religious items.

4. The first seven days of mourning after a death are referred to as *shivah*. Traditionally, the mourners refrain from normal activities, sit on benches, rend their clothing, go barefoot, and cover their heads. They spend their time with friends and family and perhaps read a few appropriate biblical passages. After these first seven days, *sheloshim* begins; it is a period of lesser mourning lasting thirty days. The bereaved widow or widower cannot remarry or go to celebrations or any kind of festivity. After these periods were over, a return to normal daily functions and habits was urged, in order to discourage excessive mourning.

Glossary

Attestat zrelosti: "Certificate of maturity," equivalent to French baccalaureate (Russian)

Bar mitzvah: Ceremony at age thirteen which marks a boy's manhood by reading the *Torah* before the congregation (Hebrew)

Bentsh licht: To bless and light the Sabbath or festival candles (Yiddish)

Bris: Circumcision ceremony held eight days after a boy's birth, symbolizing entry into covenant with God (Hebrew)

Bubbe: Grandmother (Yiddish)

Challeh: Braided loaf of white bread made for the Sabbath (Hebrew)

Chanukah: The festival of lights (Hebrew)

Chazan: Cantor or reader who chants or sings prayers in the synagogue, leading the congregation (Hebrew)

Cheder: Elementary level of Hebrew school for boys (Hebrew)

Chumash: Pentateuch, the first five books of the Old Testament (Hebrew)

Chuppah: Canopy under which bride and groom stand when their marriage is formalized (Hebrew)

Collège des jeunes filles: Secondary school for girls (French)

Daven: To pray (Yiddish)

Dorf: Village (Yiddish)

Duma: May refer to a municipal council which elects a mayor as well as to the national parliament (Russian)

Externi: A student studying for an educational degree through an examination (Russian)

Feltsher: A medical assistant without university training (Russian)

Flayshig: Meat/poultry (Yiddish)

Folkschule: School, often organized by those sympathetic to socialism, which taught secular Jewish culture and Yiddish (Yiddish)

Furgon: Covered wagon (Russian and Polish)

Galach: A negative term for priest (Hebrew)

Gefilte fish: Fishcake made (often for Sabbath) from chopped cod or whitefish (Yiddish)

Gemara: A part of the *Talmud*; often used to refer to the whole *Talmud* (Hebrew)

Get: Bill of divorce (Hebrew)

Gildikupets: Merchant guild in Russia (Russian)

Goy (plural, *goyim*): Gentile (Hebrew)

Grueneheim: "Greenhorn," a recently arrived immigrant (Yiddish)

Gymnaziia: Secondary school (Russian)

Hasid: Member of a sect of Orthodox Jews (Hebrew)

Hegdesch: Jewish hospice for the poor, supported by the community (Hebrew)

Imenie: Estate (Russian)

Istino russkii: "True Russian" (Russian)

Kaddish: The prayer for the dead or a son who will say the *kaddish* (Hebrew)

Kantseliarskii: Office (Russian)

Kasheh: Cooked groats (Yiddish)

Kest: The right of a newly married couple to live with the bride's family after marriage, especially if the husband is a scholar (Hebrew)

Kibbutz (plural, *kibbutzim*): An agricultural cooperative settlement in Israel (Hebrew)

Kiddush: A prayer said on Friday evening over a goblet of wine to sanctify the Sabbath (Hebrew)

Kind (plural, *kinder*): Child (German)

Kosher: (Adjective) Refers to the dietary regulations adhered to by strict Jews. (Verb) To salt and soak meat in a prescribed manner (Hebrew)

Krupa: Grain dish, like groats (Russian and Yiddish)

Kugel: Noodle or potato pudding (Yiddish)

Landsman (plural, *landsleit*): Someone from the same place in the Old Country (Yiddish)

Landsmanshasten: Organization of *landsleit*, often for mutual benefit and recreation (Yiddish)

Macher: Big-shot; wheeler-dealer (Yiddish)

Matzoh: Unleavened bread eaten during Passover (Hebrew)

Mazel tov: Good luck (used to congratulate) (Hebrew)

Mikveh: The ritual bathhouse, one for each sex; a married woman should go for ritual purification after menstruation and childbirth, and a man might go after seminal emission or for ritual purity before the Sabbath or holidays (Hebrew)

Milchik: Dairy (Yiddish)

Minyan: The quorum of ten male Jews necessary for religious services (Hebrew)

Mujiks: Peasants (Russian)

Nadan: Dowry (Hebrew)

Nogid: Respected community leader who uses his wealth for charity, who mediates disputes, and otherwise conducts himself in an exemplary manner (Hebrew)

Pale of Settlement: Area to which Jewish in Russia were legally restricted (see map)

Parakhod: Steamship (Russian)

Payrich: Ethics of the Fathers, a book of ethical maxims and epigrams, a tractate of the *Mishnah*, read on Sabbath afternoons between Passover and *Rosh Hashonah* (Yiddish)

Pesach: Passover, the eight-day holiday in the spring commemorating freedom and the escape from Egypt (Hebrew)

Pidyon haben: Redemption ritual of the first-born son of a woman (Hebrew)

Pogrom: Anti-Semitic riot (Russian)

Prifstok: Captain (Russian)

Purim: A joyous spring holiday celebrating the defeat of the tyrant Haman and the saving of the Jews recounted in the book of Esther (Hebrew)

Rabbi: In the Old Country, a teacher (Hebrew)

Rosh Hashonah: Jewish New Year, which comes in the fall (Hebrew)

Rov: Fully ordained graduate of a theological university (Hebrew)

Seder: Ritual meal for Passover (Hebrew)

Sepharim: Books, any books of traditional learning, but especially the scrolls of the Torah (Hebrew)

Shabbes: The Sabbath; Saturday, the day of rest (Hebrew)

Shabbes goy: Gentile hired to do essential chores on the Sabbath, when Jews are forbidden to work (Hebrew)

Shammes: The sexton for the congregation, who also acts as the *rabbi*'s assistant (Hebrew)

Shaygets (plural, *skutsim*): Male Gentile (Hebrew)

Sheloshim: The thirty-day period of lesser mourning, which follows the first seven days after a death (Hebrew)

Shiddach: An arranged marriage (Hebrew)

Shiksa: A female Gentile (Hebrew)

Shivah: The first seven days of mourning after a death (Hebrew)

Shlep: To drag along (Yiddish)

Shochet: Ritual slaughter necessary to provide *kosher* meat (Hebrew)

Shtadlan: Intercessor (Yiddish)

Shtetl (plural, *shtetlach*): A small town whose population is mostly Jewish (Yiddish)

Shul: Synagogue (Yiddish)

Simchath Torah: The last day of *Succoth*, celebrating the ending of one cycle of *Torah* reading and the beginning of the next (Hebrew)

Succoth: The festival of Tabernacles in the fall (Hebrew)

Talmud: Books of commentaries on the *Torah*, including *Gemara* and *Mishnah*; contains the rabbinic legal heritage of Judaism (Hebrew)

Talmud Torah: Religious school (Hebrew)

Torah: Narrowly, the first five books of the Old Testament; broadly, all traditonal Jewish lore (Hebrew)

Trakhoma: Trachoma, an eye disease (Russian)

Trayf: Everything not *kosher* (Yiddish)

Tzedaka: Righteousness by charity, good conduct, and compassion (Hebrew)

Verein: An organization of people from the same area in the Old Country (Yiddish)

Yeshiva: An institution for higher religious learning (Hebrew)

Yeshiva bucher: A *yeshiva* student personifying all the stereotypic attributes —shyness, unworldliness, etc. (Hebrew)

Yichus: "Pedigree" referring to family tradition of philanthropy, scholarship, and respected occupations (Hebrew)

Yom Kippur: The second of the High Holidays, the Day of Repentance (Hebrew)

Yontif: A holiday (Yiddish)

Zhandarm: Policeman (Russian)

Zhid: A derogatory term (like kike) meaning "Jew" (Russian)

Bibliography

Aleichem, Sholom, *Tevye's Daughters*, translated by Frances Butwin (New York: Crown, 1949).

———— *Stories and Satires*, translated by Curt Leviant (New York: Thomas Yoseloff, 1959).

Anderson, Mary, *Woman at Work*, as told to Mary N. Winslow (Minneapolis: University of Minnesota Press, 1951).

Antin, Mary, *The Promised Land*, 2nd edition (Boston: Houghton Mifflin, 1969).

Asch, Sholem, *The Mother* (New York: Liveright, 1930).

Cahan, Abraham, *The Rise of David Levinsky*, Commentary edition (New York: Harper & Row, 1960).

———— *Yekl and the Imported Bridegroom*, new edition (New York: Dover, 1970).

Chagall, Bella, *Burning Lights* (New York: Schocken, 1946).

Dawidowicz, Lucy, editor, *The Golden Tradition*, paperback edition (Boston: Beacon Press, 1968).

Dreiser, Theodore, *Sister Carrie* (Cleveland: World, 1927).

Ets, Marie H., *Rosa: The Life of an Italian Immigrant* (Minneapolis: University of Minnesota Press, 1970).

Handlin, Oscar, *The Uprooted* (Boston: Little, Brown, 1952).

Hindus, Milton, editor, *The Old Lower East Side* (Philadelphia: Jewish Publication Society, 1969).

Malamud, Bernard, *The Fixer* (New York: Farrar, Straus, 1966).

Manners, Ande, *Poor Cousins* (New York: Coward, McCann & Geoghegan, 1972).

Metzker, Isaac, editor, *A Bintel Brief* (New York: Ballantine Books, 1971).

Olsen, Tillie, *Tell Me a Riddle* (Philadelphia: Lippincott, 1961).

Richardson, Dorothy, "The Long Day," reprinted in *Women at Work*, edited by William O'Neill (Chicago: Quadrangle, 1972).

Richter, Ida, *Compassion* (Chicago: privately published, 1973), available from Ida Richter, 6933 North Kedzie Avenue, Chicago, Illinois 60645.

Rischin, Moses, *The Promised City* (Cambridge: Harvard, 1962).

Rosten, Leo, *The Joys of Yiddish* (New York: McGraw-Hill, 1968).

Roth, Henry, *Call It Sleep*, paperback edition (New York: Avon, 1964).

Roth, Philip, *Portnoy's Complaint* (New York: Random House, 1969).

Schoener, Allon, editor, *Portal to America: The Lower East Side, 1870–1925* (New York: Holt, Rinehart, and Winston, 1967).

Sennett, Richard, *Families Against the City*, (Cambridge: Harvard, 1970).

Smuts, Robert, *Women and Work in America* (New York: Columbia, 1959).

Wirth, Louis, *The Ghetto* (Chicago: University of Chicago, 1928).

Yezierska, Anzia, *The Bread-Givers* (Garden City: Doubleday, Page, 1925).

_____ *Children of Loneliness* (New York: Funk and Wagnalls, 1923).

Zborowski, Mark, and Elizabeth Herzog, *Life Is with People* (New York: Schocken, 1952).